Bernardino Ochino, Constance E. Plumptre, John Ponet

The Tragedy

Reprinted from Bishop Ponet's Translation out of Ochino's Latin Manuscript in 1549

Bernardino Ochino, Constance E. Plumptre, John Ponet

The Tragedy

Reprinted from Bishop Ponet's Translation out of Ochino's Latin Manuscript in 1549

ISBN/EAN: 9783743335615

Manufactured in Europe, USA, Canada, Australia, Japa

Cover: Foto ©ninafisch / pixelio.de

Manufactured and distributed by brebook publishing software (www.brebook.com)

Bernardino Ochino, Constance E. Plumptre, John Ponet

The Tragedy

THE TRAGEDY

BY

BERNARDINO OCHINO

REPRINTED FROM BISHOP PONET'S TRANSLATION
OUT OF OCHINO'S LATIN MANUSCRIPT
IN 1549

EDITED WITH INTRODUCTION AND NOTES

BY

C. E. PLUMPTRE

GRANT RICHARDS
9 HENRIETTA STREET, COVENT GARDEN
1899

INTRODUCTION

OF this very rare book the British Museum is in possession of two copies, each of which is precisely the counterpart of the other, save that in the one —inserted between the end of the Seventh and commencement of the Eighth Dialogues—there is a woodcut, representing the condition of the wicked at the Day of Judgment, with the words, "*And then shall be uttered*[1] *whom the Lord shall consume with the spirit of His mouth, and shall destroy with the appearance of His coming, even him whose coming is after the working of Satan,*" the Pope and cardinals being conspicuous among those sentenced to perdition. The other copy, from which this woodcut is absent, contains, once in the dedication and twice in the play itself, allusion to the Lord Protector, the Duke of Somerset; no such allusion occurring in the copy with the picture. Both copies bear the same date, 1549, and there is nothing to show which of the two

[1] *Uttered*, a Middle English word for *put forth* or *expelled*.

The Tragedy

was published first; whether, that is to say, the Lord Protector's name has been cancelled or added. He is known to have been a somewhat ardent Protestant, and also a very ambitious man; one not likely to allow the boy king to take much precedence over himself; and thus it is probable that the omission of his name in the dedication of a book so strongly associated with the important movement of the Reformation would have displeased him, and it might have been thought more politic to add it in subsequent copies. On the other hand, we must not forget that 1549 was the year of the Protector's downfall, and that after the occurrence of this event it would have been impossible for any book to be jointly dedicated to Edward the Sixth and to himself; in which case (and I incline to think this the greater probability) the Protector's name must have been cancelled. I have selected the copy dedicated to him in conjunction with the king as being to this small extent the completer; while at the same time I have caused to be inserted as a frontispiece a facsimile of the woodcut representation of the wicked at the Day of Judgment, from the other copy.

As I consider fidelity to the text to be an editor's chief duty,—especially with the first reprint of a work so rare as this,—I will here briefly state the very few instances in which I

The Tragedy

have ventured to add to or tamper with the text of Ochino's *Tragedy*.

(1) The play is entirely wanting in those descriptive terms *exit* or *enter*, so familiar to the reader of ordinary dramas at the appearance or disappearance of any of the *dramatis personæ*. These, when really necessary for the better comprehension of the play, I have ventured to insert. And on one occasion I have divided one of the *Dialogues*, or what we should now call *Acts*, into two *Scenes*, because a certain interval of time is evidently intended to have elapsed between the commencement and end of the Dialogue. In Ponet's translation there is no division of Acts into Scenes, but in this one instance, in which I have ventured to make the division, it seemed really necessary for the better comprehension of the play.

(2) For a work written in the sixteenth century, this play is singularly free from that coarseness of expression which, while it carried with it no sense of impropriety two or three centuries ago, has grown to be very distasteful to our own age—coarseness which abounds in Shakespere, and from which even the authorised version of the Bible is not free. Occasionally, though very rarely,—not more than three or four times in the whole play,—coarse expressions occur in *The Tragedy*, and when they do so, I have thought

The Tragedy

it better to suppress them, or supplement them by others more in accordance with modern taste. I have done this, partly, because I think it possible that this play may excite more than a scholarly interest. In the present state of religious agitation in this country, it seems not improbable that it may attract religious notice, may enter into religious households, and be read by the young as well as by their elders. In each case the alteration is purely of a verbal nature, in no way obscuring Ochino's meaning, or detracting from the vigour of his language.

With these two exceptions, this reprint is an absolutely faithful copy of the original, save that the black letter type has been here replaced by modern printing, and the spelling of the sixteenth century has been changed into that of the nineteenth; black letter printing and sixteenth century spelling both being a little confusing to the unaccustomed eye. But when I have come across any obselete or obscure word I have invariably reproduced it, giving its modern equivalent in a footnote. The notes at the bottom of the page are alone mine; those on the side margin—pertaining chiefly to scriptural references—are either Ochino's or his translator's. I have been at some little pains to discover what edition of the Bible Ochino or Ponet referred to in these marginal references, and I think it is that which

The Tragedy

on the binding bears the names of *Tyndale* and *Coverdale* and dated 1549, but on the inside is described as *Matthews' Bible* of 1538, being an improved edition of that of 1537. The chapters are divided not into numbered verses, as with our authorised version, but into alphabetical paragraphs, letters being used instead of numbers. These I have allowed to stand as they are, and I have also given the old form of the spelling of scriptural names, such as *Esay* for *Isaiah*; because, if any reader should happen to be in possession of that rare prize, a Matthews' Bible, or not possessing it, may care to verify the references at the British Museum, he will more readily be able to do so. The only reason I have for not deciding quite definitely that this must have been the edition used, is that when there are any allusions to the Book of Revelation in the "Tragedy" they are invariably expressed by the abbreviation *Apoc.*, signifying Apocalypse. But in no Bible that I have examined in the British Museum does the Book of Revelation go by the name of Apocalypse, save in the Table of Contents. It is, of course, possible that Ochino may have consulted some foreign manuscript edition of the Bible, and that his translator rendered his references into the English version of Matthews.

On the title-page *The Tragedy* is described as "never printed before in any language." Ponet

The Tragedy

must consequently have translated it from Ochino's manuscript. This manuscript does not seem to be in the possession of the British Museum; and I need scarcely say that the difficulty of editing this reprint is to some extent increased thereby. It is quite impossible, for instance, to rectify the typographical errors by any reference to the manuscript; or again, to judge whether the courtly phrases in praise of the Lord Protector—so common at this period from author to patron—are Ochino's or Ponet's. In face of any evidence to the contrary I am inclined to say that they are Ponet's, who seems to have been far less single-minded and unworldly than Ochino.

Before proceeding to give a short biographical notice of the author of *The Tragedy*, it seems fitting that I should devote a few lines in description of its translator, which I base chiefly on the articles devoted to him in *Chalmers' Biographical Dictionary*, and the *Dictionary of National Biography*.

John Ponet or Poynet was born, according to Chalmers, about 1516, while the author of the article in the *Dictionary of National Biography* names 1514 as the probable year of his birth. He was educated at Cambridge, and became especially skilled in Greek; but he knew also mathematics, German, Italian, and astronomy. He was a strong supporter of the Reformation,

The Tragedy

but probably as much from politic reasons as from any higher motives; for he was somewhat unscrupulous in his public actions, while his domestic relations seem not altogether free from reproach. But he was undoubtedly a very able man and of versatile talent. In early life he seems to have been quite a remarkable mechanist, constructing a clock which pointed to the hours of the day, the days of the month, the signs of the zodiac, the lunar variations, and the tides. It was presented to Henry VIII., and considered by him an extraordinary production. Cranmer, seeing his ability, selected him for his chaplain. In the year 1549 Ponet made the translation of Ochino's *Tragedy* that is here reprinted. It brought him to the notice of the Lord Protector, and the following year he preached the Friday sermons before Edward VI. Honours soon gathered round him. Bishop of Rochester, and Bishop of Winchester, he was one of those entrusted with the responsible task of making a new code of ecclesiastical laws. When Mary came to the throne Ponet was deprived, and is said to have fled to the Continent. There is a tradition that he took an active part in Wyatt's rebellion. Eventually he found his way to Peter Martyr at Strasburg, where he died in 1556.

Bishop Ponet is of course chiefly interesting here as the translator of Ochino's *Tragedy*. As I

The Tragedy

have already said, there is no copy of the manuscript of this play in the British Museum. It is impossible, therefore, to say how far this translation is accurate. But my readers will probably agree with me that, whether accurate or no, or whether it was undertaken from motives of religion or from motives of policy, it is singularly free from that common fault of translations: it does not read like a translation. Taking it as a whole, it is devoid of those cumbrous, involved sentences which so often make translations a positive burden to read. It will, I think, be granted, that the English rendering by Ponet of this play is couched in the terse, vigorous, lucid language so eminently characteristic of English literature at this period.

Bernardino Ochino was born at Siena, a short distance from Florence, in the year 1487, just four years after the birth of Luther. He was of a strongly religious bent, and, like most religious youths in that period, was powerfully attracted to a religious life. He selected that rule of the Friars of St. Francis called the Observants, because of the unusual severity with which it was credited; and in 1524 he was made General of the Observants. But he was not satisfied with his Order. Self-indulgence rather than austerity was what he saw daily, and there was but little discipline. Longing for a greater reality in his religious life,

The Tragedy

he threw aside the dignities that he had attained to in the rule of the Observants, and resolved to pass as a simple friar into the Order of the Capucin. Here, too, he soon rose to distinction. He was endowed with a great gift of oratory, and in this character attracted the notice of the Emperor, Charles V.

But even in his new Order Ochino could find no resting-place. In the sixteenth century the Church of Rome was almost at her lowest ebb; and as he gradually acquired a knowledge of the widespread immorality that seemed to pervade the members of all the Orders alike, Ochino began to lose faith in the Roman Catholic system. In 1542 he left Italy and went to Geneva. Here he seems to have adopted opinions more or less Lutheran; at times preaching justification by faith, and employing the language of extreme Evangelicalism; at others veering towards Socinianism, and teaching that not even Christ should be allowed to come between a man's soul and his God. Like Luther also he took unto himself a wife. In 1547 he came to England, and remained there six years; and it was in England, two years after his arrival, that he wrote *The Tragedy*. From this time his fortunes were more or less adverse, though his persecution seems to have taken no severer form than exile, and banishment from his various places of refuge.

The Tragedy

It is impossible to read Karl Benrath's *Life of Ochino* without seeing that the author of *The Tragedy* was a man of great conscientiousness and single-mindedness. His revolt from the Papacy arose wholly from moral reasons. To use his own words, he had "not forsaken the Church, but only the impiety and superstition which falsely assumed for itself the title of Church ; and I have forsaken it not that I may proclaim false doctrines with impunity and lead a licentious life, but that I may recognise the truth and practise Christian discipline."[1] Believing firmly in a Moral Providence, the Mystery of Evil pressed upon him profoundly for some interpretation—as it has pressed, and still presses upon most thoughtful minds. Seeking for some solution of this profound Mystery, he endeavoured to find it, as it had been long previously attempted to be found, by the writer of the Book of Job, and has been, subsequently to *The Tragedy*, attempted by Milton in his *Paradise Lost*, and by Goethe in Faust—all of which deal with various forms of the same great subject—in the interpretation that this great evil of the Papacy could only have arisen from the direct instigation of the Evil One himself. In his *Life of Milton*, in the Great Writer Series, Dr. Richard Garnett has drawn attention to the remarkable parallelism between

[1] Karl Benrath's *Life of Ochino*, translated by H. Zimmern, p. 129.

The Tragedy

Ochino's *Tragedy* and Milton's *Paradise Lost*; so great indeed that, though the *motif* of the one is the Fall of Man, and of the other the Rise of the Papacy, it is difficult to believe that Milton was unacquainted with the earlier work, though he nowhere mentions it.

The *Tragedy* is undoubtedly an indictment, couched in language of extreme severity, against the Church of Rome. In these more tolerant days, it is probable that no one would think it quite justifiable to attack any religion, however alien from his own way of thought, with such undisguised animadversion. In justice to Ochino, it must be remembered, that at no time within living memory has the Papacy even faintly approached the extreme of moral obliquity so rampant in the sixteenth century, and that consequently the same necessity has not arisen; moreover, although he was so unsparing with his pen, Ochino nowhere advocates persecution. By the mouth of Edward VI., as one of the *dramatis personæ* of *The Tragedy*, he speaks thus:[1] "To drive him (*i.e.* the Pope) out of the hearts of men it is not needful to use sword nor violence. The sword of the Spirit, that is, the Word of God, is sufficient." For one living at a period when Protestants almost equalled Catholics in their ardour for persecuting all who differed from them, it is, I think, greatly

[1] See p. 247 of this book.

The Tragedy

to Ochino's credit that he not only refrained from advocating persecution, but that he was wise enough to recognise the folly and uselessness of it; seeing that, as is common with most violent forms of opposition, it generally succeeds in bringing about what it would fain prevent. As he makes Lucifer say in the First Dialogue : " When we kill one Christian man there springeth, as it were of the ashes of him, a hundreth immediately in his place. When we intend to bring the kingdom of Christ to nothing then we make it more noble, rich, and glorious."[1] The only weapons sanctioned by Ochino in religious disputes in *The Tragedy* are those of fair argument and fearless exposure of any iniquity inseparably associated with the system under discussion. "As soon as he (the Pope) hath once lost his spiritual kingdom in men's consciences," he makes Edward VI. say, "he shall forego by and by all the rest of his jurisdiction."[2]

It is, I think, quite possible to feel sincere respect for individual Roman Catholics, and yet to deprecate, almost as strongly as Ochino himself would have deprecated, any attempt to bring back —even in a modified form—the Papacy, as a system, into Protestant countries. Nor is it necessary to adopt all the views of extreme Evangelicalism, as advocated in *The Tragedy*, in order to regard with distrust the reactionary wave that

[1] Pp. 3, 4. [2] P. 247.

The Tragedy

is spreading just now over the country. The student of the history of the Papacy, the student of social science, the man of the world who has travelled much in Catholic countries, the humanist, or man of letters, who knows full well how greatly learning suffered when the Papacy was at the height of her power; all, I think, can sympathise with the zealous Protestant in his desire to resist by all fair and lawful means any attempts at encroachment on the part of the Papacy into this country.[1] In the words of the late J. A. Froude, " All brave men are Protestants who refuse to take a lie into their mouths in the name of religion."

There is a wise Egyptian proverb which says, *The Mother of Foresight looks Backwards.* Such of the younger generation now amongst us, who are beginning to lose appreciation of the immense privilege of the liberty of private judgment, wrought for them primarily by the Reformation —for which privilege their fathers fought and bled—and are learning to crave instead for some sure refuge in the shape of priestly authority, can hardly take a "backward look" that should prove of greater profit to them than this portrayal, in *The Tragedy*, of the Papacy at the height of her power; when authority had her full sway, and any attempts at private judgment were suppressed as if they were a deadly sin, as indeed at that time they

[1] *Lectures on the Council of Trent*, p. 106.

The Tragedy

were so regarded. The "backward look" into this drama should prove all the more efficacious, when it is remembered that *The Tragedy* was written by one who was for years in closest association with the Church of Rome; who was bound to her by the tender ties of ancestry and environment; who had little to gain from writing of her as he wrote, but, on the contrary, had a good deal to fear.

C. E. PLUMPTRE.

August, 1899.

To the most mighty and most excellent Prince Edward the Sixth, by the grace of God, King of England, France and Ireland, defender of the faith, and in earth Supreme Head of the Church of England and Ireland, Bernardinus Ochinus Senensis wisheth all felicity.

Although God of His mere[1] goodness hath given to your Majesty most rich treasures, most large kingdoms, special grace and love of all people, most high nobility of blood, most singular ornaments both of the body and the mind, partly coming only of God, and partly through His favour obtained also by your industry, beside other innumerable graces, which it hath pleased God to endue your Highness withal: Yet nevertheless all these things ought not, cannot be compared to that benefit, which He hath showed unto you, in giving unto you in such a dark world, and in so tender age, such clear light of Christ, that albeit in this world He was poor, low, despised, and crucified, and your Majesty is so rich, so high, in so great honour and all kinds of felicity. Yet not only you acknowledge and take Him for your Lord and Master; but also you love Him, and that in such sort, that for the love which you bear unto Him, you have such a godly hatred to His enemies, that following

---

[1] *Mere*, absolute, entire.

The Tragedy

the blessed memory of your father, first with the favour of God, and then with the advice of your most dearest uncle, the Lord Protector, and of other your trusty and faithful councillers, you have driven out of your realms and dominions him, who among all the wicked hath the highest place, and is most adversary to Christ, and therefore is he, and may worthily be called, Antichrist. Now remaineth nothing behind, but that with him you drive away also, as you have begun, his lies, errors, hypocrisy, simony, robbery, superstition, idolatry, and all wickedness. And then if Pyrrhus, Alexander Magnus, Hannibal, Scipio Africanus, and Julius Cesar had noble victories and triumphs in this world, how much more shall your noble acts far pass all them and their acts in the sight of God, angels, and men, forasmuch as you (being yet but almost a babe) shall overthrow the most mighty, most crafty, most wicked, and cruel tyrant that ever was, or ever shall be in the world, delivering your subjects from a long and miserable bondage and captivity.

And yet, forasmuch as many (such as be blind and do take him for their god on earth, whereas they ought most highly to commend your Majesty for your godly proceedings) peradventure will speak evil of so excellent an act, I thought it my part, for the duty that I owe to God and to your Majesty, to show unto such men the beginning of this their Papacy, and how it increased, and came into so high estimation among the blind people: so that they, perceiving their weak, false, ruinous, and devilish foundation, may leave their faith which they have in him, and give glory to God, and to your Majesty, to whom I pray God to grant a most long and blessed life.

The Tragedy

The parties that do speak in these Dialogues are these :—

　　I. Lucifer and Beelzebub.

　　II. Boniface the third, and Doctor Sapience, Secretary to the Emperor.

　　III. The People of Rome—The Church of Rome.

　　IV. The Pope—Man's Judgment and the People of Rome.

　　V. Thomas Massuccius, the Master of the Horse. Lepidus, the Pope's Chamberlain.

　　VI. Lucifer and Beelzebub.

　　VII. Christ, and Michael and Gabriel, Archangels.

　　VIII. King Henry the Eighth and Papista, and Thomas, Archbishop of Canterbury.

　　IX. King Edward the Sixth and the Lord Protector.

A Tragedy or Dialogue of the unjust usurped primacy of the Bishop of Rome, and of the unjust abolishing of the same, made by Master Barnadine Ochine, an Italian, and translated out of Latin into English by Master John Ponet, Doctor of Divinity.

A tragoedie or
Dialoge of the vniuste vsurped primacie of the Bishop of Rome, and of all the iust abolishyng of the same, made by master Barnardine Ochine an Italian, & translated out of Latine into Englishe by Master John Ponet Doctor of Diuinitie, neuer printed before in any language.

Anno Do.
1549

To face page 1.

I

LUCIFER AND BEELZEBUB

LUCIFER. My dear faithful brethren, and most entirely beloved friends, forasmuch as I know how much profit ariseth of the labour and pains that ye take in the world, be ye well assured that I would not have willed you to assemble here together in Hell at this present were there not some great profit to our commonwealth arising of the same that moved me so to do. Ye know right well, my brethren and friends, how wrongfully and unjustly our enemy God (without our own fault or deserving) hurled us down out of Heaven headlong, and also ye know what grievous torment, misery, and calamity we have sustained ever since that time. And although He will needs reign alone in Heaven, and can abide no fellow to be joined with Him in that kingdom, but doth usurp it whole to Himself alone; yet if He would have left to us some dominion in earth, this torment and misery of ours might better have

Esay xiv.,
Luke ix.,
Apoc. vii.

The Tragedy

been borne. But whereas we had by much travail and business obtained and enjoyed, as it were by our prescription, of many years the dominion of the world, see you not how He hath sent this same Son of His, whom they call Christ, to mar all that ever we have made, and utterly to destroy that we John xvii. have builded; do ye not perceive how that fellow Christ, being nailed upon the cross, draweth all men unto Him; and do ye not perceive what a number of men which before were of our side be now fled to Him, there to be soldiers underneath His banner. If His apostles, being but twelve, made such a commotion through the whole world, what a rustle, think ye, will so many thousands make, whom they, by their teaching, have turned? Certainly, by conjecture, it should seem that the matter will daily wax worse and worse, unless this great mischief be wisely provided for in season, else will it at length come to pass that our sceptre royal shall be plucked out of our hands, and our dominion utterly taken away from us. But after long consulting and devising there is now come into my head a very handsome imagination, whereby we may destroy the kingdom of Christ and establish our kingdom for ever. If we attempt to oppress the members of Christ with persecution and tyranny we shall that way but increase more and more our own sorrow. For, as we be sufficiently taught by long experience, they be so

The Tragedy

possessed and led with a zeal to the glory of God, and so carried with a vehement, heavenly spirit, that they contemn all things, saving Christ only. And this one thing seemeth much to be marvelled at, that when they be spoiled for the glory of Christ, or banished into exile, or lose their honour, their country, their substance, yea, or their life also, yet they earnestly triumph and be merry, and they esteem it as a game won, and a joyful victory to suffer all kinds of misfortune for Christ's sake, so that the more sorrow we do unto them the more glorious and famous they be, and we remain in more misery and confusion. Comp. with Gala. vi., Phil. i.

And, again, there is one other thing, both more hurtful to us and more to be lamented; that is, the rest of the people perceiving them to bear such ignominy and rebukes with so marvellous patience, so joyful hearts, and so constant a courage, be compelled to think thus with themselves and say: Truly God liveth and worketh in them marvellously; if they had not an experience and a taste (by a secret moving of the Holy Spirit) of another life in Christ, much better and happier than this present is, they would never be so desirous to be rid of this present life. And if it so be that we kill one Christian man (as the fable is of the cutting of one of the heads of Hydra, the serpent) there springeth, as it were, of the ashes of him a hundred immediately in his place. John iii., Phil. i., Gala. ii., Heb. xiii., 1 John v.

The Tragedy

When we intend to bring the kingdom of Christ to nothing, then we make it more noble, rich, and glorious. Now if we should attempt to overcome this our ancient enemy's kingdom by reasons and arguments, we shall do nothing else but increase our own rebuke and shame. No man can withstand their wisdom, wherewith, if our reasons be compared, truly they be very foolishness. Therefore it is expedient and necessary, seeing that we cannot overcome them in plain field with open war, to attempt their overthrow by art, policy, diligence, craft, subtlety, guile, and prodition.[1] I have conceived in my head a deceit of such weight and importance that if I may bring it about after such sort as I have devised it, there was never man saw, neither yet in the world was there ever any that devised the like, both for the strangeness and for the force thereof. I have devised with myself to make a certain new kingdom, replenished with idolatry, superstition, ignorance, error, falsehood, deceit, compulsion, extortion, treason, contention, discord, tyranny, and cruelty; with spoiling, murder, ambition, filthiness, injuries, factions, sects, wickedness, and mischief, in the which kingdom all kinds of abomination shall be committed. And notwithstanding that it shall be heaped up with all kinds of wickedness, yet shall the Christian men think that to be a spiritual

[1] *Prodition*, treachery.

The Tragedy

kingdom most holy and most godly. The supreme head of this kingdom shall be a man which is not only sinful and an abominable robber and thief, but he shall be sin and abomination itself, and yet, for all that, shall he be thought of Christian men a god in earth, and his members, being most wicked, shall be thought of men most holy. God sent His Son into the world, who for the salvation of all mankind hath humbled Himself even to the death of the cross; and I will send my son into the world, who for the destruction and condemnation of mankind shall so announce himself that he shall take upon him to be made equal with God. This is our counsel and witty invention, and it is not to be doubted but that if the matter come to pass as I would have it (as my trust is that it will be) we shall in short space see a revenging of that our old injury.

Matt. xv. c and ix. b; Luke xix. a; John xii. f, xiv. 6; I Timothy i. a; Phil. ii. a.

BEELZEBUB. When I behold you, most redoubted prince, and ponder your words generally with myself, ye would not believe how much I am comforted. Methinketh that I am now so satisfied, and that I feel myself so presently eased, as though I myself had poured out all the boiling poison of my stomach against God. There was never creature that had a more witty, a more noble, or a more worthy device, if the matter might take like effect, as meseemeth it cannot. For who could believe that the Christian men

The Tragedy

(which excel in wisdom and judgment) could be brought to this point to believe that the kingdom of the devil is the kingdom of God ? and that the supreme head of that kingdom, being the very great Devil of Hell, ought to be adored and worshipped for a god in earth, and his members honoured for saints?

LUCIFER. Oh how goodly occasions many times men lose, and how goodly enterprises come not to such effect as they were purposed for, by the means of the weak fearfulness of men's stomachs, in that they dare not take the thing in hand, which they be afraid they shall not achieve! Such as be of hault [1] courage advance their mind, studying and attempting things of great adventure, and so with wit, industry, diligence, care, and earnestness, at the last they bring things to pass that be very hard to compass. My hope is, therefore, that even as God hath saved the world by Christ, so in spite of Him I shall destroy the same, and that under the pretence and colour of the same Christ, by the means whereof men may be the easier deceived. I will stir up the chief captains of my kingdom, that they may so by craft and diligence shadow and cover superstition and idolatry with a fair face, and beauty of feigned holy ceremonies and of good intent (as they call it), that men shall be made so

---

[1] *Hault*, literally haught or haughty, but meaning here high or lofty.

The Tragedy

drunken and so amazed with this outward pomp and show that they themselves shall not be able to discern truth from falsehood, when they be drowned in the midst of the flood of idolatry and superstition. Moreover, I have determined so to extol and set up the carnal man in this my kingdom, and the light of nature and the strength of man's free will and his works, that I shall be able to cast down Christ out of His place and to bury His great benefit, and so to diminish the profit of His grace, His righteousness and merit everlasting. And furthermore I will bring men into that madness that they shall think themselves not only able by their own power and might to enjoy the praise of righteousness before God, but also that the election and choice of their salvation shall depend wholly upon themselves. All these things will I persuade to men under a pretence of a more perfect righteousness and honesty, under a shadow of a better setting forth the glory of the name of God. And although the principal heads of this kingdom be full of darkness, of ignorance, of heresy, error, fraud, and lies, yet shall they shamelessly take upon them the usurpation of authority to make new and wicked articles of the faith, wresting the Holy Scriptures to their crooked purpose; and yet shall they think themselves to be in a great clearness of light and truth. For I can easily persuade unto them that their Church is the

The Tragedy

Church of Christ, although it be nothing else indeed but a very assembly of Satan. I will persuade unto them that they be the disciples of Christ, and the successors of St. Peter, when indeed we be their chief masters, and they our vicars, and supply our ruins and serve our cures in earth. Finally, when indeed we reign in them, they shall think they have the Holy Ghost within them; so that although they be in a continual error, yet shall they persuade men that they are inspired with a heavenly spirit and cannot err. Oh Lord![1] what a number of mischiefs and abominations shall be committed in this kingdom by reason of the wicked and sinful decrees which shall be made of governors of the same, when they shall glory that they have power to bind the conscience of men even of like sort, as though they were hail-fellow with God, or rather better, and all this under the shadow of religion and holiness. I will cause them to be most cruel tyrants and butchers of Christ and His chosen members, and that under a pretence of a zeal to the house of God. They shall attempt to hide their uncleanness under a gay name of fool-

---

[1] *Oh Lord!* According to Mr. Knight, the well-known editor of Shakspere, in the sixteenth century, this expression, *Oh Lord*, had not grown into the half-humorous, half-vulgar phrase of modern life, but was used in all earnestness. Ochino, therefore, probably intended to represent Lucifer as using it in no mere slight exulting mockery, but in intense malignant hatred and revenge. The modern equivalent of the expression *Oh Lord!* of the sixteenth century, would probably be *My God!*

The Tragedy

life;[1] and shall cover their wickedness and abomination with an exceeding wide cloak of hypocrisy, and with a glorious shining title of religion and holiness. But what needeth so many words? The chief head of this kingdom shall be directly quite contrary to Christ, and the members of it shall be open adversaries to the chosen of God. But one thing, my friends, ye must diligently consider that this thing of necessity be always kept secret; else, if men should perceive by any means this our counsel, all our labours should be lost and all our enterprise frustrate. Doubt ye not, dear brethren, but that if this thing come to pass that I intend, there shall be such horrible and wicked viciousness in this kingdom that the chief captains themselves could not abide them if they knew them to be so abominable as they shall be. Wherefore it is necessary that the greater the wickedness shall be, the more craftily and cunningly they be announced and set forth with some pleasant, beautiful face of religion, and a gay painted veil of holiness.

BEELZEBUB. All these things we allow right well, and be also ready to obey your counsels and to bestow all the powers of our wit and might to set forward this noble enterprise. Howbeit, first and foremost, we think it very expedient that ye dis-

[1] *Fool-life*, probably Fool's Paradise, a name signifying, in the sixteenth century, indulgence in unlawful pleasures. Thus in *Romeo and Juliet*, Shakspere makes the nurse say to Romeo, 'If ye should lead her (Juliet) into a fool's paradise, as they say, it were a very gross kind of behaviour.'

The Tragedy

close plainly unto us all your intent and purpose, that we may direct all our labours and study to that end, and so to bring this noble enterprise about even as we will, with the common consent of us all.

LUCIFER. Even as upon Christ dependeth the whole salvation of all mankind, so is it necessary for us to devise a supreme head upon whom may depend the whole condemnation of all mankind. And as the Son of God for the salvation of the world did abase Himself from the high state of His divinity, and endued Himself with man's nature : of a like sort is it needful for the destruction of the world that there be some man which shall announce himself above Christ and above God Himself, that men, being blinded by stinking and filthy superstition, may fear, honour, and obey a mortal man more than the living Lord. And, moreover, it is necessary that this man be so furnished with all wickedness and iniquity that I may worthily say of him : This is my beloved son in whom is my only delight, hear him ; even as the heavenly Father long agone did testify of His Son Christ.

BEELZEBUB. Methinketh that I hear the lively image of Antichrist himself, handsomely and properly described of you.

LUCIFER. It is even so, indeed, as thou sayest.

BEELZEBUB. But who is, I pray you, so shameless to receive so wicked a dignity ?

The Tragedy

LUCIFER. 'Receive it,' quoth he! This dignity shall be honoured and set forth with so much riches, so much pleasure, and so much abundance of things; so greatly befriended with noble men, so decked with honour and great wealth of this present life, that all the princes of the earth shall be desirous to attain thereunto. And as for the abominations of this high seat, they shall be so covered with a gay, glorious outward show of holiness, that they themselves which shall sit in the same shall not be able to know their own wickedness. No (a man would scarcely believe it), they shall think themselves very gods in earth. As far as my wit will serve me, I think the Bishop of Rome the most meet instrument to bring about the thing that we intend. Because that Rome is the head city of the world, it shall be no hard thing to persuade men that the bishop thereof is the head of all Christian men, and the Church of Rome to be mother of all other churches. And again, the insatiable ambition of the Romans, their craft and malice and guile, wherewith they be naturally infected, shall not be the only thing that shall help forward our purpose; but also the favour and grace that they obtain at the Emperor's hands of Rome. Furthermore, it is not unknown unto you that, by reason of the manifold heresies which we have sown in Africa and in the East parts of the world, what a number of bishops have

The Tragedy

fled to Rome for succour of the Emperor. The Bishop of Rome (as a man that gapeth for this honour of the highest place) entertaineth all men very friendly, declaring tokens of kindness and love towards everybody, insomuch that some of a mere simplicity, and other some by craft and fraud, will be so desirous of the election and appointment of this high dignity that they will be very glad to give their voice to the Bishop of Rome; who, on the other part, is so replenished with deceit and subtlety, and with such a bottomless desire to be a prince, that it shall be easy for him with the help and favour of our spirit to attain to this most high dignity, namely[1] because, as ye know, they be sufficiently furnished already with learning, and also helpers by the power and working of our spirit. The churches of the East part of the world were easily infected with the heresies that were sown abroad, and because their heresies be now known to all men they cannot infect the other churches of Christ, which be more sincerely instructed. But as for this Church of Rome, it must be infected by little and little, not in the outward show, but in the inward bowels; and that so extremely that it cannot be made more wicked (the outward pomp and show and a certain form of the Church of Christ being preserved), that by the means thereof it may bring all other

[1] *Namely*, particularly.

The Tragedy

churches more easily into error, and may be the only chief breeding mother of error and wickedness, like as it shall be taken for the mother of all other churches. Thus have I declared unto you, dear brethren and friends, all my whole invention and imagination; and I have opened also and set before your eyes the end whereunto we must direct all our labours and study. It resteth now with you that every one apply his whole mind to the uttermost of his power for the performance of so noble an enterprise, and leave nothing undone that shall seem expedient for the bringing about thereof. Doubt ye not that the time is at hand when we may revenge our old injury against God; and forasmuch as He would not suffer us, being most worthy creatures, to be fellows with Him in Heaven, we will bring to pass by our industry that the vilest man and most castaway in the world shall be above Him on earth. And now that every one of you in his degree may the more cheerfully apply himself about this business, I promise you, ye need not doubt, but you may be well assured, that we shall in short space bring the thing to pass that we desire. For in this point we have God Himself favourable unto us, Who in sundry places of Scripture prophesied that there should an Antichrist come; and now is the time expired wherein that wicked head of Christendom ought to come into the world. Then, if God

<small>Esay xiv.,
Luke x.,
Apoc. xii.</small>

<small>Matt. xxiii.</small>

The Tragedy

will not be made a liar, it is necessary that at the last he come and be disclosed to the whole world. For with this whip God will scourge and punish the false Christians; who, because they would not believe the truth, God of His rightful judgment will that they shall believe lies, and be worthily deceived, as Paul hath written. There were never, nor never shall be, more shining ceremonies, nor more beautiful, whereby to allure men under a colour of holiness, than those shall be which Antichrist and his members shall devise to be used among men. And know ye, moreover, for a confirmation of their doctrine and living, that they may be more easily deceived, God will suffer many wonders, many signs and miracles, to be showed by us, by reason of whom even the very chosen shall be seduced, if it were possible, as Christ Himself hath prophesied. I am sure ye have in remembrance how, that in the beginning of the Church of Christ when it was most pure, and a long season after, there were chosen as well in Rome for to be bishops such men as were most godly, best learned in God's Holy Scriptures, and as most diligently and faithfully laboured to announce God's true word and His glory; but afterwards when good discipline began to decay, and when we had poured ambition, darnel,[1] and dissension into

---

[1] *Darnel*, a kind of worthless grass, but used here somewhat as "tares" is used in the parable.

The Tragedy

the world, then were chosen to be bishops, by their own procurement, not such as were most godly, but such as were most worldly, most ambitious and crafty, seeking more their own glory and lucre than the announcement of God's glory and the exercise of their office, rather plucking from the sheep their milk than feeding them with good pastures. So that the name of a bishop now is no more the name of a very painful office, as it was in times past, but of a great pomp and dignity. Furthermore, they have ordained, according to the example of the old Patriarchs, Abraham, Isaac, and Jacob, three new Patriarchs: one of Antioch in Asia, another of Alexandria in Africa, and the third of Rome in Europe.[1] Of a like sort, ye know that a long season all Christian men in the Church of Christ have been taken for spiritual, sanctified, and religious men, as they be called in the Scripture, and as they are indeed, forasmuch as they be hallowed in baptism and dedicated to God to be His children and to be led by His Spirit. But the infidels, which be not of the Church of Christ, as men utterly without Christ, be accounted (as they be indeed) profane, heathen, and ungodly. But now of late days only a sort of cloisterers,[2] disguised men in apparel, and living from other

---

[1] In the text 'Europe in Rome,' but this must evidently be an error in transcribing or printing.

[2] *Cloisterers*, men living in cloisters, or monks.

The Tragedy

men, begin to be taken for spiritual, religious, and holy men, though they be never so vicious. All other Christian men, be they never so godly, and replenished with the heavenly spirit, yet be they judged profane, and unworthy to touch their garments with their little finger. This wonderful dignity and magnificence shall set out the royalty and glory of our monarchy not a little. Believe me, dear brethren, we have a meet time and opportunity for our triumph, for our glory and victory. God, for the announcement and for the increase and establishment of His Church, gave to it the Holy Scripture for a rule to live by for ever; likewise for the increase, the enlarging and confirmation of our Church, we will give unto it our decrees and canons, which, although they be for most part profane and wicked, yet shall they nevertheless not only seem good and holy, but also they be taken for the very squire [1] and rule whereby the Holy Scripture shall be tried. Furthermore, because God knew right well that His Holy Word is a thing most necessary above all other, He commanded His apostles that they should preach throughout the world the voice of the Gospel, which indeed is the true chief office of them

---

[1] *Squire and rule*, square and rule, methods or instruments of measurement. In the sixteenth century, *square* was often written as *squire*. Thus Spenser in the *Fairy Queen* says:

> Temperance, saith he, with golden squire
> Betwixt them both can measure out a meane.

The Tragedy

which will be taken for the true ministers of Christ. For although baptism (as all men know), be a ceremony ordained of God both holy and necessary, yet was the Apostle Paul so diligent and busied with preaching the Word of God that he christened very few with his own hands, but left that office to other ministers. But now shall the time come, yea, and it is at hand, wherein the chief heads of this our kingdom shall not only challenge[1] to be the successors of the apostles, but also of Christ Himself; they shall be stricken with such a madness that they shall think it a vile, shameful thing for them to preach the Gospel, and therefore shall they substitute under them simple Sir Johns,[2] who for the fashion's sake shall pretend and do the outward ceremony of preaching, but the doctrine wherewith they shall instruct the people shall be handled and infected after their own fashion. And as for the bishops, they shall be given altogether to esteem things of the world and of the flesh. And yet to the end that they may appear before men as though they were bishops indeed, at certain times of the year they shall set forth sundry ceremonies with a great show to the people, which shall be no less cold, dumb, and foolish than wicked and superstitious, which shall be framed and wrought in our workhouse of Hell. But briefly to comprehend an

---

[1] *Challenge*, lay claim to.   [2] *Sir Johns*, a common name for priests.

The Tragedy

endless sea of matters in few words, know ye, my brethren, that this kingdom of ours shall be so pestilent and abominable that it shall not only infect and hurt the Church of God, the holy ceremonies and constitutions, true worshipping of God and the sacred Scripture itself, but it shall also destroy and overthrow other liberal arts and sciences.

BEELZEBUB. When I consider how short the life of man is, it seemeth to me a thing impossible that one Bishop of Rome, in so short a space, should bring to pass so many mischiefs.

LUCIFER. Brother, methinketh that ye be very dull. For this name of Antichrist is not the proper name of any one man, but is a common name to many; for notwithstanding that it is a fit name for all of them that be contrary and enemies to Christ, yet chiefly and above all others it agreeth to those Bishops of Rome which usurp tyranny, lordship, and dominion above all other bishops. Now all the difficulty and hardship of this business standeth in the beginning thereof, that is to say, in giving a beginning to a matter of so great importance, and that same Bishop of Rome may be found who dareth give the first adventure to be called the head of all other bishops. If we may once obtain this at one of their hands, the rest will easily follow willingly; and daily will they find out new ways for the establishment of their dominion.

The Tragedy

Therefore let us all go now out of hand, and every man prepare himself to do his endeavour, according to his calling. I, as your chief captain, will first prove a foremost attempt to persuade this godly imagination of mine to Boniface, the Bishop of Rome, and I doubt not but that I shall obtain favour of his carnal wisdom.

II

BONIFACE THE THIRD—DR. SAPIENCE, SECRETARY TO THE EMPEROR

BONIFACE. Oh immortal God, how sweet and pleasant a thing is the glory of the world ! Truly it is more to be esteemed than all worldly treasures or pleasure. I am the Patriarch of Rome, and have under my tuition and governance an infinite number of people ; who, being pressed with any kind of affliction, straight they come running to me as thick as hoppes ;[1] they all honour me ; they have their eyes set upon me. I have money at will, and I may have all kinds of pleasures at my command. Yet if I could bring it to pass to obtain at the hands of Phocas, the Emperor, the dominion and principality over all other bishops of the world, I would think myself to have attained even the very highest state of felicity and happy life that might be. If then I

---

[1] *Hoppes*, a Middle English word for grasshoppers, locusts, and creatures of a like nature that *hop*. Probably locusts are intended above, as they always come in swarms.

The Tragedy

could not by wisdom and industry bring to pass that men should worship me as a god in earth, I might worthily be accounted as a fool, and much unworthy of so great a felicity. But what shall I do? I can by no means disclose this my phantasy to any man, but I shall forthwith disclose this mine arrogancy, and he shall judge me a man of ambition. But I see Master Sapience the Emperor's secretary, mine old friend. Truly I could not have found a more fit instrument for my purpose: if he will be so good to me as to open this thing to the Emperor's Majesty, not as a thing devised and found out of me, but rather of his own head, as though I durst not hardy[1] of my head, will, or mind so great a matter. [*Enter* SAPIENCE.]

SAPIENCE. God save your highness, most reverend Father.

BONIFACE. Ye be very heartily welcome. What news?

SAPIENCE. Nothing but that all is nought. Sundry letters there be brought to the Emperor's Majesty, the contents of the which doth declare that there is such a number of factions, sects, contentions, and of divers kinds of heresies in the Church of Christ that without God's present help the Church will shortly be bitterly undone.

BONIFACE. Your words give me both occasion

The communication between Boniface, Bishop of Rome, and Dr. Sapience, the Emperor's secretary.

---

[1] *Hardy*, to venture or hazard.

The Tragedy

and encouragement to disclose unto you, as to my most faithful and dear friend, my whole mind and intent. I will therefore open unto you the secret and hid purposes of my mind. But because the matter is of great weight, first I will desire you to keep counsel.

SAPIENCE. Sir, that is a thing that belongeth to mine office, to keep secrets; forasmuch as I am secretary to the Emperor's Majesty, a dignity whereunto I should never have attained, if I had not somewhat learned what thing it is amongst men privily or openly to wist or to talk. Wherefore be not afraid; say what ye will, and think with yourself that ye may safely say your mind to me; for assurance whereof I promise you faithfully that I will open it to no man, neither speak anything thereof to any man living, but as you shall be contented.

BONIFACE. For one epistle and one message that the Emperor hath received of factions and heresies, which abound in Asia and Africa, I have received a thousand letters and messages; for all good men resort to me as their only refuge and succour, and I comfort them in their afflictions and calamities. There be many also, not all of the best sort, which resort to my guard and tuition; some lest they should worthily be punished of their superiors for their offences; and other, that under the shadow of my favour they may be promoted

The Tragedy

to some dignity. And I of very humanity and gentleness cannot but entertain them very friendly, and show all tokens of kindness unto them, be they good or be they evil that come to me for refuge. It is not ambition that moveth me to this thing, neither go I about by this means to increase my private commodity,[1] or to advance the worthiness of my dignity (as God, He knoweth); but Christian charity and a true zeal to God's honour moveth me to do this my duty. Unfortunate had the Christian men been which dwell in those countries had I not holpen them with my labour and diligence! There is none among them who desireth not the increase and setting forth of mine honour, that my authority and help may be a stay unto them in such things as belong to their profit. But I of a certain natural inclination (I cannot tell how) both naturally and willingly abhor all pomp and dignity. Yet to say as I think, and as my conscience giveth me to speak the truth, I fear me much lest all churches, not only they of whom I spake even now, but our churches also, in short space will be undone, unless they be governed of some universal supreme head. Ye know right well, that where is no order, there of necessity must be confusion; neither can there be any certain order except there be a head, whereunto all things must be applied as to the chief state of governance.

[1] *Commodity*, advantage.

The Tragedy

And to put you out of doubt, Christian men be not now of that simplicity and virtuous behaviour as they were in the beginning of the Primitive Church, wherefore now it is necessary for them to have a head which may punish the evil and reward the good. Ye see with your eyes how many sects and heresies be now in the Church of Christ, and there is small likelihood of amendment, but that it shall be daily worse and worse. If some remedy be not found betimes, shortly shall ensue amongst men such a licentious and unbridled liberty that every man will attempt to invent a new kind of religion of his own brain, so that every man shall believe what him listeth, and shall also refuse whatsoever shall seem contrary to his private commodity. Wherefore it is very necessary that there be some supreme head to reduce all men to an unity in religion, whereby all waves of opinions may of a Christian sort be calmed and ceased. Experience, which deceiveth no man, but is the chief mistress in consultation, teacheth this thing so evidently that it cannot be denied. Now that we have by sage conjecture espied it to be necessary to have one head in the Church and Christian commonwealth, I judge that Christian men will more willingly and readily admit and receive me for their head and governor than any other man ; which thing may be compassed both more safely and better without business, if the Emperor would

The Tragedy

help it forward (being so profitable a thing as it is) with his royal authority; against whose will and pleasure as I dare attempt nothing, so would I not doubt but that if he would do this thing himself, it were no small means to increase his glory, and establish the continuance of his memory for ever, and also for the enlarging of his imperial dominion and dignity. For if I should acknowledge perpetual obedience, reverence, and fidelity to him (as I am bound, and as my mind is to do), he might well think all the dominion and authority which I should have to pertain also to him. Now if you think it good to commune with the Emperor's Majesty in this matter when ye shall see time and place convenient (because I know that he loveth you singularly well and that he setteth much by your counsel, and I know how good ye be to persuade a matter, and also I am well assured that ye be my very friend), I doubt not but ye shall easily bring to pass this my desire. And for my part, besides that I should be always bound unto you, I would declare unto you, indeed, after no slender and mean sort, how earnestly I love you for that I had received so great a benefit at your hands. And I will be plain with you: my desire is that ye will open all these things to the Emperor's Majesty as though they were first devised by you, and as though I had never talked nor spoken of them. For methinketh it a wisdom, when I have

The Tragedy

obtained my suit, to show myself as though it were against my will, that I might say amongst all men that I take not this dignity willingly, but by force and compulsion.

SAPIENCE. I perceive all that your highness hath in this plentiful oration declared, and I promise you my faith and true diligence for the compassing of this matter, and that my good heart and mind shall appear to your highness to be void of all dissimulation. And as soon as I shall perceive what answer Cæsar's Majesty will make, I shall declare his will and pleasure to your most noble lordship; and because I am now even cloyed with so many businesses, and am also sure that there be a great number looking for me at the Court, I will take my leave of your highness, unless ye will command me any other service.

BONIFACE. Nothing but that ye will humbly commend me to Cæsar's Majesty.

SAPIENCE. I will with all my heart. [*Exit* BONIFACE.] I thought the time of my tarriance[1] with this man to be a whole year long: he displeased me so with such a rolling rhetorical vanity of words. Oh Lord God, that there can be so much ambition and desire of honour hid in the breast of a man, and that of a Christian man, yea, and of a bishop, which will be accounted most holy! It is no marvel that he entertained so

[1] *Tarriance*, stay or tarrying.

The Tragedy

friendly all strangers that came to Rome, and oftentimes praised them earnestly to the Emperor, for it appeareth by the matter itself that it was for none other purpose but to obtain the favour of his neighbours and strangers for the better attaining to this dignity which he hunteth for. And to cloak his hypocrisy with a gay outward show, he saith it is very necessary for the Church to have one supreme universal head of the Church in earth, as though Christ were not the true head of His Church, or else did not regard things in earth, but sat in Heaven idle and sleeping. He affirmeth also that if this head be not established in the Church of Christ it will shortly decay and be undone; but I am of a contrary judgment. If Cæsar's Majesty fulfil his ambitious desire, the Church of Christ will not only decay, but it will utterly fall down as though it were plucked up by the roots. As though the bishops which be already were not sufficient for the churches that they have! And if there chance any contention to arise amongst them, they have counsels by whom to make an end of their strife and controversies. What knowledge can this false wretch have of the churches in Africa, or of the churches in Asia, where he was never in all the days of his life? But what talk I of Africa and Asia? How can he govern those churches that be in Europe, whose language for the most part he understandeth

The Tragedy

not, by the reason of the great distance of places and variety of the nations and men? Who ever saw one crane guide all other cranes in the world? Who ever saw a shepherd which could alone feed all the sheep in the world? He were worthy praise if he could govern his own well, though he were not a whit troubled with caring for the rest. Who knoweth whether wolves may be found in his own flock, and whether he may worthily be judged the chief wolf of all? It is not many years agone since John, Bishop of Constantinople, attempted the same enterprise, that he might be made the universal bishop, whom the whole Church did withstand, and namely [1] Gregory the First, this man's predecessor, who in his letters, amongst other things, wrote unto him: That the name of a universal bishop was a foolish, wicked, proud, and a church-robbing name, and if he should go about to usurp that name he should do nothing else but make himself like to Lucifer, and be a foremessenger of Antichrist, in taking away the glory and dignity from other bishops, his brethren, and so to trouble the concord and unity of the faithful, and undo the Church of Christ. Now if this ambitious fellow may by craft and subtlety obtain that thing, which his predecessors, with the common praise and consent of all men, did most justly condemn in other,

[1] *Namely*, particularly.

The Tragedy

surely it shall not be done without great offence of all good men. This I dare be bold to say, that neither Africa, neither Greece, neither the rest of the Churches of the East, will ever consent hereunto, but will rather resist and rebel amongst themselves; and so shall the seamless coat of Christ be torn in many parts. This shall be the first fruit which shall spring of this devilish state and authority. Furthermore, the churches either will not consent thereunto, or else if they do consent it shall be by compulsion, because they may easily perceive how much mischief this marvellous tyranny shall bring with it. If all the tyrants which ever have been were joined together, they all never did so much mischief to the world as this one is like to do. I see plainly that this matter is a thing most pernicious and hurtful, whereof I ought neither to think nor speak, but only to put away so great a mischief from Christian men's necks. Yet because I have made promise, I will see what the Emperor will say to it, and will talk earnestly with him of the matter; forasmuch as this ambitious bragger did declare plainly that he would see me well rewarded, if I would do that lay in me to help the matter forward. Besides this, because he is named to be our countryman, one of the Romans, I am bound to promote his suit and purpose. And who knoweth what he will do shortly after for my

The Tragedy

sake, if he obtain this dignity by my procurement? Truly it is not like that he will forget so great a benefit received at my hand. Nay, the more they strive amongst themselves the more shall they need the Emperor's help, with whom I am chief, and so my vantage shall be the fatter. Therefore will I bring this thing about, and that with as much celerity and speed as possible. [*Exit* SAPIENCE.]

SCENE II[1]

BONIFACE. Since I disclosed my mind to Dr. Sapience I have been wonderfully troubled. And who knoweth whether he will (in so weighty a matter as this is) keep counsel or not according to his promise? He hath a number of friends whom he will put in trust with some of my matters. And what if he open somewhat of my will in declaring the matter to the Emperor? But be it that he do none of these things? Yet can it not be but that Cæsar's majesty of himself (as he is replenished with wisdom and exceedingly practised in such kind of feats) shall by and by suspect that this arrow came out of my quiver, and that the matter was altogether of my devising; and so my craft shall be espied and I put to shame. Furthermore, if it so chance that he obtain not my suit at the Emperor's hand, what have I then

[1] In the text this Dialogue runs on without any division into Scenes.

The Tragedy

else done but disclosed unto him my bottomless ambition to no purpose? But if he obtain (as I pray God he may), all men will say with one accord that I have brought it to pass with much labour and industry, and so shall the thing be left in writing to the posterity. And so shall I be both to men of this present age, and to them which shall be in time to come, a laughing-stock and a jesting-stool. All men, good and evil, will have their eyes set upon me, and (as it were) point me out with their finger. I shall be hampered in a thousand snares. And one thing is greatest mischief of all: I alone shall be the first beginner and the chief original of all the abominations which my successors shall commit in all the whole world by the reason of this tyranny. But why trouble I myself any longer with a rabblement[1] of reasons? The die is cast, happen what happen will: and I cannot, saving mine honour, draw back again from my purpose; therefore methinketh it more meet to stand to the matter stoutly, tarrying to see the end. If the matter come to pass as I would have it (as I trust it will), I will find a means quickly how I may find friends plenty. The matter of itself telleth, and daily experience showeth, that all men hunt for the friendship of them who excel in riches and authority, although they be very

---

[1] *Rabblement*, crowd or multitude.

The Tragedy

tyrants. And to the intent that men shall the more embrace and magnify me, thinking me to be a Christ on earth, I will cause it by letters to be blown abroad over all the world that this high dignity chanced to me, both not looking for it, and altogether unwilling to receive it, and that I would have received it in no wise had not the zeal that I have to the house of God compelled me; that is to say, to provide a remedy for heresies, factions, and an infinite number of other mischiefs by the which the Church of Christ is oppressed. But Master Sapience is come, and his journey is towards me with speed. He seemeth very merry; no doubt he bringeth me some good news. [*Enter* SAPIENCE.]

SAPIENCE. Your most reverend highness should not marvel that I have deferred and prolonged the time for answer to the matter which I know to be to us both very pleasant, longer than either of us both did suppose. Truly the cause why I did was no negligence, but rather that I might bring the thing to pass more diligently and more effectuously.[1] I chose my time and place when I might best for our profit declare this matter to the Emperor. Yesternight after supper methought His Majesty was merrier than he was wont to be; he walked forth into a garden, and being there alone he called me to him apart. There he began to declare unto me his power, his riches, and to

[1] *Effectuously*, effectively.

The Tragedy

extol and magnify the greatness of his empire and dignity, and further he opened unto me certain secret counsels whereby he thought to increase his riches and to cause his whole dignity royal to be the more esteemed. And I, perceiving this thing to make somewhat for our purpose, did not only confirm and approve his intent, but also added this thing moreover: that he now had such occasion and opportunity given him to increase his honour as never other emperor had before him, so that he would speak but one word. Now because these words pleased him wonderfully, he desired me earnestly to declare unto him how and by what means this thing might be brought to pass. Then said I : If your Imperial Majesty would attempt to subdue the dominions of other princes, ye may not think that it would be brought to pass without much bloodshed, without great danger and difficulty. But ye now have an occasion offered unto you of God, which if it will please you to take when it is offered, ye shall not only without difficulty, but also with much ease and favour of all parties, subdue all Christian regions. So that those people which be farthest off shall come and submit themselves to your Majesty gladly and willingly. When I perceived that he gave very good heed to my talk, whilst I should open this hid mystery, first I declared unto him how the Church of Christ was shaken and

The Tragedy

tossed with sundry miseries and calamities, and for none other cause but that it lacked one supreme, spiritual, and universal head in earth, whereunto all men that were afflicted with any kind of misery might resort as to a common refuge, and that all men both knew and desired this thing. I declared also how this head, for the opinion's sake of religion (whereunto all men be naturally inclined), should easily be received of all the whole world. And moreover, by reason of the thunderbolts of excommunication, it should be terrible to all nations, so that in short space it should enjoy a firm and a perfect dominion. Besides this, I showed him that if one of the Emperor's subjects should be chosen to be this supreme head, which should hang altogether upon the Emperor's will and pleasure, he should be a very meet instrument, easily to compass the dominion of the whole world. And thus I came nearer by little and little to the communication of your most reverend highness. I did put him in remembrance how much you favoured His Majesty, and how meet a man above all others ye seemed for this purpose, and again for the great estimation in that ye were Bishop of Rome, in the which Rome[1] ye did now service with high praise and

[1] The second spelling of this word is in the text *roume*, but in the sixteenth century spelling was more or less in a state of flux, and it is no uncommon thing to find the same word spelt in a variety of ways on the same page ; or it may mean, figuratively, *room* or office.

The Tragedy

commendation; and also how much this thing was desired of very many men, which should increase the renown of the Emperor's Majesty with a great rejoicing of all nations. This thing also I added: Unless His Majesty would declare and establish this head by his authority it would shortly come to pass that some others would attempt the same thing and bring it to pass, he not knowing thereof; yea, though he did gainsay it, who (to His Majesty's great shame and rebuke) would choose some other which was no subject to His Highness, but (so it might chance) his adversary and foe, that either would spoil utterly, or, at the least, much vex the borders of the Roman Empire. In conclusion, these and such-like reasons prevailed so much with him that, being persuaded, he interrupted me of my tale and spake to me before I had made an end of showing my mind, praying and beseeching me that I would go busily about this matter, and that I should come straightway to your highness in his name, and so in his name pray you very earnestly that ye would not refuse this condition thus offered, neither disdain to receive this burden whatsoever it be. And this is true also I may tell your highness in counsel: The Emperor charged me privily that I should not tell you that he desired this thing so much for the private commodity which might thereby to him ensue, but for the glory of God and the

The Tragedy

profit of the Church. Thus your highness hath the beginning, the middest,[1] and the end of my message.

BONIFACE. My dear friend, Sir Sapience, notwithstanding that the last day I communed with you somewhat hourly[2] of this matter; yet after that I had weighed it more substantially with myself, I perceived it to be a dangerous enterprise and full of peril, and so hard to compass and so painful, that I have repented me more than a thousand times since that ever I began it. So that if I could have conveniently brought it to pass in time, I would have changed my former purpose, and have desired you never to open your mouth, neither to the Emperor, neither to any man else, for this or such-like matter. This I am sure is very true, that there was some Heavenly Spirit that moved me as soon as I first spake of this matter. But now am I in such a perplexity and doubt that I wot not what is best to do. For this is once :[3] I love quietness, and my desire is to pass over the rest of my life in rest and peace without ruffling and business. And on the other side again, there is a certain zeal to the honour and glory of God which stirreth and pricketh me, neither would I willingly resist the calling of the Holy Ghost. Then cometh in the authority of

---

[1] *Middest*, middle.
[2] *Hourly*, lengthily.
[3] *Once*, first.

The Tragedy

the Emperor's Majesty, whose beck, word, and request I take as a commandment unto me. Therefore tell the Emperor how that when I thought nothing less than this thing, ye laid glory of the name of God to my charge ; and at the last when ye had proved the thing to me by exceeding strong reasons, that I could not refuse this heavenly vocation being freely offered unto me without a manifest and open injury to God's holy name, and therefore that I was compelled to receive this offer. But of this one thing I desire you to move Cæsar's Majesty very earnestly, and ye shall move it to him in my name ; that is, that he will consider again and again when I am advanced up into this high estimation I shall have many earnest adversaries, whose darts he himself must defend, and also guard and preserve me in that place wherein I am by him placed. And I think it in very deed more wisdom, and more standing with both our honours, that even at the very first beginning, neither he should grant, neither I usurp, this supreme authority for the avoiding of all tumult as much as may be. It is enough at the first that I be proclaimed chief bishop of all. And afterwards as time and occasion shall serve, we will go on farther a little and little, using dominion and authority meet for such a dignity. Therefore let him speedily cause the writings to be penned, and proclamation to be made throughout

The Tragedy

the world of this his determined mind and pleasure. Shortly after will I come humbly to see him; and furthermore I will have in remembrance how much I am bound to you, and what I have promised you when time shall require.

SAPIENCE. All this shall be done, and fare ye well. [*Exit* BONIFACE.] Even as of late our bishop disclosed unto me his wonderful ambition, so now I perceive that he hath hid within him such an hypocrisy as never was heard of. I know that he runneth mad for this dignity, and yet went he about with his crafty, glozing, and deceitful words to persuade that he would never receive it when it was offered. Now seeing that he goeth about to hide it from me, unto whom he first opened it, how will he handle other that know not his deceitfulness? Surely his shameless ambition deserveth no less but that I should let all the matter quail;[1] which thing would be very acceptable to God, no doubt. But we have waded farther herein than is easy for us to stop it, being almost brought to pass already. The Emperor himself is so amazed and drunken with my words, that by no means possibly can I withdraw him from his purpose. And I myself, who was the beginner and procurer of this matter, am forced not to forsake my suit, but rather with my judgment to allow it, and with my diligence to perform it. What shall a man

[1] *Quail*, languish or come to nought.

The Tragedy

do? Such chance doth chance to them that attempt naughty matters. I will get me hence; the sooner I bring this thing to pass, the sooner shall I be delivered of these naughty and painful fantasies.

III

THE PEOPLE OF ROME—THE CHURCH OF ROME

THE PEOPLE OF ROME. I understand by common report that the Bishop of Rome is made head of all other churches by Phocas our Emperor. If it be true, he hath done a thing more foolish, more abominable, more perilous, and more wicked than ever was either done or heard of. The Emperor knoweth not how much ambition, guile, malice, craft, and wickedness reigneth in him ; he hath begun to brood in his bosom such a young adder as will shortly shoot up to a mighty dragon, and will at length dig out his own eyes. This priestling, in continuance of time, will so grow in ambition, pride, and boasting in vainglory that he will establish his seat above the dignity of the Emperors. There will a time come, and it is now very nigh at hand, when it shall be needful for the Emperor, if he will have his crown, he shall ask it and receive it (if it please him to give it) at our bishop's hands ; and that he shall come as an

The Tragedy

humble suitor to him and kiss his feet, and he (in the name of God), a very holy bishop, shall tread with his foot upon the Emperor's throat. Neither will he be contented with all that ignominy, but in conclusion will strike off his head. Ye may chance peradventure that the Emperor's name only shall remain unto him, but he shall not possess one foot of land which shall properly be called the Emperor's. Oh lamentable state of thee, Oh people of Rome! What misery art thou falling into! Thou shalt be taken from a great dominion and noble renown, wherein thou didst flourish in times past, and shortly shalt be made a driven drudge and a vile slave of a most foul castaway priest. If our old, ancient, noble-hearted Romans should live in these days, how would they abide it when they should see the sacred Senate-house replenished with so many wicked thieves! But I see the Church of Rome coming out of the Church of St. Lateran. She seemeth to journey towards me, and I desire very much to commune with her. I have met her in good time. [*Enter the* CHURCH OF ROME.] God save you, Holy Church of Rome!

THE CHURCH. Wish ye me to be saved when as I within these few days have gotten so much salvation and health by the reason of the wonderful dignity that I have received at the Emperor's hands, whereby I am the mother of all other churches, that the health of all the whole world

The Tragedy

dependeth upon me? Therefore must not I receive this thing of other, but communicate it to all other.

THE PEOPLE. Since I understood that our bishop is changed by the Emperor from Most Reverend to Most Holy and Most Blessed, I have been more troubled than ever was man, and many and sundry doubts doth vex my brain.

THE CHURCH. Show me your doubts, and I will resolve you fully in them all; for ye know right well that there is nothing to be doubted of my answer. I am now made blameless, so that I cannot err.

THE PEOPLE. Tell me in good faith, had ye never a beginning?

THE CHURCH. Yes, without question.

THE PEOPLE. And who was your mother that conceived you?

THE CHURCH. The Church of Jerusalem, as it was forespoken by Esay[1] the prophet. The law came out of Sion, and even so the Word of God from Jerusalem. Therefore when Christ ascended into Heaven there remained none other Church in earth besides the Church of Jerusalem, and she, by the ministry of the apostles, begat all other churches.

THE PEOPLE. If the Church of Jerusalem be your mother (as ye confess her to be), how then

---
[1] *Esay*, Isaiah.

The Tragedy

cometh it to pass now that the selfsame mother is made your daughter?

THE CHURCH. Oh Immortal God! what a gross philosopher ye seem to be! For even as ye know right well that the selfsame Virgin Mary is both the mother and daughter of Christ, even so am I myself the daughter of the Church of Jerusalem, and also the mother of her and all other churches.

THE PEOPLE. Oh how blind was I! Now I perceive how the matter standeth. As the Virgin Mary is the carnal mother of Christ, and also Christ's daughter spiritually, so be you; whereas in times past ye were the spiritual daughter of the Church of Jerusalem, within this few days ye are made the carnal mother of the same Church and all others. Now then, seeing ye be the carnal mother of all churches, ye shall as a carnal body be shortly infected, and so infected that in short time ye shall deprave and destroy with your poison, rottenness, slander, and corruption, all other churches as well as yourself. And when they all be once poisoned as ye be, ye shall beget them to Hell, as in times past the Church of Jerusalem, your spiritual mother, begat you to Christ. Surely I marvelled how ye could otherwise regenerate the Church of Christ (which is governed with the Spirit of God, else is it not the Church of Christ), except ye gave unto it the spirit of the devil, for there is but only One Holy Spirit which continueth for ever.

The Tragedy

THE CHURCH. I will be their spiritual mother, and as a spiritual mother I will comfort them, give suck to them, and nourish them to Christ.

THE PEOPLE. Nay, ye will suck all the blood from them, and if ye fortune to give them suck, it shall be with the milk of adulation and flattery.

THE CHURCH. I will make all churches rich.

THE PEOPLE. Yea, wise with jubilees, pardons, and blessings.

THE CHURCH. I will defend such as fly to me for succour when they be oppressed with each other.

THE PEOPLE. Ye will defend them indeed, be it right or wrong, if they bring money.

THE CHURCH. If there arise any doubt in matters of religion, I will open it by-and-by.

THE PEOPLE. With your own judgment against the Word of God.

THE CHURCH. I will also punish them that will not obey.

THE PEOPLE. Ye may with your wicked decrees and decretals, and that with fire, whereunto ye will commit them which confess the wholesome doctrine of the Gospel, which is quite contrary to your doctrine. I deny not but ye may be so high above other churches in spirit, in faith, and good works, and so much profit them with your good example and learning, that ye may worthily be called their mother and superior ; but I am afraid lest altogether chance clean contrary, and that there was

The Tragedy

never tyrant so cruel towards his subjects as you will be towards your daughters, and therefore not worthy to be accounted or called their mother.

THE CHURCH. Be it that I were as wicked as might be possible, yet shall I always be their mother, for that one prerogative the Emperor himself hath given unto me.

THE PEOPLE. And what power, I pray you, hath the Emperor to make you mother of other churches, if they agree not amongst themselves thereunto, but be all utterly against it; namely[1] the churches of the East, in countries where the Emperor hath no power nor dominion? It must needs be, therefore, that ye confess the Emperor hath the chief authority in spiritual matters, and even as he gave you this dignity wrongfully, so may he lawfully take the same away again from you.

THE CHURCH. Nay, that will I never grant, were it never so true. Fain would I have you persuaded in this point. Even as the mother, after she hath conceived and brought forth a child, she is always the child's mother, be she never so evil, neither can the Emperor cause her leave off to be a mother, or make her not to have had a child whom she hath brought forth, because that thing is once done and past; after a like sort, after that I am once made the mother of all other churches,

---

[1] *Namely*, particularly.

The Tragedy

and that by the Emperor's authority, the Emperor cannot bring it to pass with all the power he hath that I shall not be evermore the mother of them whom I have begotten.

THE PEOPLE. And how may it be that you have begotten all churches, when it is evident that there was a great number before you, yea, and that you were begotten of other?

THE CHURCH. Oh brainless head! knowest thou not that when Christ hung upon the cross and showed John to His mother, and said, Woman, behold thy son, so that after those words once pronounced, forthwith he was made her true and natural son; so that after those words once pronounced, it shall be always true that John was born of her. Now of the same fashion, when the Emperor showeth unto me all churches and saith, Behold thy daughters, by-and-by am I made their true, lawful, and natural mother. And then began this sentence first to be true, that they were all born of me, and therefore can it not be but that I begat them and am their mother for ever.

THE PEOPLE. Christ, by this word, minded to declare nothing else to His mother but that she should from thenceforward take John instead of her son, and that he should take Mary instead of his mother, as he always did; but His mind was not that she should be John's natural mother as she was that conceived and bare him.

[margin: John xix.]

The Tragedy

THE CHURCH. Lo! now ye come in with your tropes and figures. The words of Christ are simply to be understanded. Christ said to His mother, Behold thy son, and He said to John, Behold thy mother; so that it followeth well, Mary was John's very true mother, and John was Mary's very true son; but how this may be behoveth us not curiously to search. Of a like fashion the words which Christ spake at His last supper when He there ministered to His disciples, taking bread into His hands and delivering it broken to them that sat with Him, saying, This is My body, be simply and plainly to be understanded; that is to say, that the bread is the very body of Christ, and not the bread is a figure of the body of Christ: of the very same fashion the Emperor's words must be understanded plainly as they stand; wherefore I conclude that they be my true lawful daughters, and I am their mother.

THE PEOPLE. What! when you never begat them? I neither knew, neither could believe, that the Emperor had ever any such authority, that he could make that thing to be done, which was never done in this world; that is to say, that he could make you bring forth those churches which ye never brought forth. If the Emperor have so great power that he can make those things to have been which were never, no doubt he can bring to pass also that those things were never which have

The Tragedy

been, and so may he cause also that ye never were, neither even shall be their mother. This would I learn of you: when the Emperor said unto you, Behold thy daughters, what thing was it that he showed unto you?

THE CHURCH. All churches.

THE PEOPLE. The Churches of Christ or the Churches of the Devil?

THE CHURCH. I am indifferent.

THE PEOPLE. If it be as you say, I think he showed unto you the Churches of Satan. As touching my part, I dare boldly say there is no cause why I should rejoice in this dignity, but rather lament; for whereas I was your only son and heir, now when ye have a many of daughters, and ye must give to every one of them their dowry, so that I shall remain a beggar.

THE CHURCH. Nay, thou shalt be richest of all others. Know ye not the fashion of the Turks, which selleth their daughters for a certain sum of money to them that shall be their husbands? so will I sell my churches and bishoprics to them that will give most money; and so shall the spoil of all other provinces come immediately to Rome.

THE PEOPLE. Then will ye commit simony, and nourish a den of thieves.

THE CHURCH. I told thee afore that I cannot err, and so must thou believe if thou wilt be

The Tragedy

accounted my son, yea, although thou sawest me commit daily all kinds of abomination.

THE PEOPLE. This cannot be, except I lose my five wits.

THE CHURCH. Nay, I would ye should not only be persuaded that I cannot err, but also that I am most holy, and ought to be called most holy after such a sort that he which nameth me holy and not Most Holy is to be thought not to speak of me.

THE PEOPLE. Then when the apostles in the Creed say, we must believe one holy church, we must not think that saying to belong to you. But I heard say not long agone, a thing more to be wondered at, that our bishop is made most holy of all and most blessed of all other above God's name.

THE CHURCH. Thou hittest the nail on the head.

THE PEOPLE. Then as concerning holiness he shall be superior to Christ, who by the authority of Scripture is named Holy of Holies. But this good blood of ours is called by the mouths of men Most Holy. Therefore should he not desire to come into heaven. For be it that he were there even now, more than blessed should he not be. Wherefore he should not ascend to a higher state of felicity but rather descend to a lower. And it is marvel if angels and saints which be in Heaven come not with speed to Rome and there begin to

The Tragedy

sue for this dignity of the Bishopric of Rome, that they may be made more blessed and more holy than they now be. I heard, moreover, that he is declared the head of all other churches.

THE CHURCH. So it is, indeed.

THE PEOPLE. Had not then the mystical body of the Church a head before now? If it were so, it might well be accounted monster-like. And I marvel very much how it could live.

THE CHURCH. Oh, Christ was the head.

THE PEOPLE. Then the Emperor hath taken away Christ and put our bishop in his place.

THE CHURCH. Nay, not so; but he hath joined the head to the Church, and yet doth Christ remain.

THE PEOPLE. That talk is more shameful. Was not Christ able to govern His Church as an universal head? In the beginning of the Primitive Church, and a little while after, the Church of Christ did flourish very much, and was wonderfully replenished, and yet had it none other head but Christ. He only as a true head did govern it, and that exceedingly well, by the instruments of His ministers. May it come to pass at any time that Christ, being wearied with His painful governance, would now rest Him, so that He now hath committed it to the Emperor's discretion to appoint some suffragan and helper in His stead? Or else truly is He much displeased

The Tragedy

with His Church and loveth it no more, neither regardeth the governance thereof, but withdraweth His Spirit from it, and so shall be a liar in that He saith: I am with you to the world's end. Furthermore, the Emperor, as it appeareth, is more careful for the Church of Christ than God Himself. For when God withdrew Christ from His Church the Emperor hath provided it another head. But, according to the doctrine of Paul, we be not ignorant that the militant congregation of Christ is as one body whose head is, was, and ever shall be Christ Himself. He as the only true head hath governed it hitherto singularly well, and will also govern it until the latter day of judgment, and even until such time as He hath subdued His enemies and put them under His feet. Think ye that Christian men be such bussards[1] that they will believe Christ and His Spirit to be taken away up into Heaven as into a place appointed for His Majesty, and is there contained as a triumphing head of a triumphant Church? And for that cause the Emperor hath appointed another head of the Church Militant in the stead of Him that is absent? Yet if it be so, ye must of force grant that the selfsame head, forasmuch as it is destitute of the Spirit of Christ, hath the spirit of the devil, and so it shall be a devilish head. And if the Church Militant shall

Matt. xxviii.

---

[1] *Bussards*, buzzards or blockheads.

The Tragedy

from henceforth have two heads, surely it shall be a thing like a monster. Neither can I perceive by conjecture how two heads, being equal in power and most contrary in condition, may quietly and safely live together, and govern at one time one special charge. Verily it is to be feared (so wonderful is the pride of our bishop bred by the bone) that he will drive Christ out of doors from His own kingdom. But, peradventure, this thing is true: if our bishop be once made supreme head of the Church Militant, by the means whereof he may be esteemed above Christ, it may so be that he will suffer after a sort that at the leastways he may use his service as he were a slave. But I can never be persuaded that he will suffer himself by any mean to be taken for an underling to Christ.

THE CHURCH. Think not that his power hath any end. For even as all power in heaven and earth is given unto Christ, so is it likewise given unto him.

THE PEOPLE. Yea, and further also, both in Purgatory and in Hell. But speak no more of his power, for surely he will take more upon him than I would wish. Another doubt I have whereunto I would have you answer me if ye can. Shall he be a common head to all churches?

THE CHURCH. Yea, verily.

THE PEOPLE. Of late I learned of them that be seen in logic, that particular men be those which

The Tragedy

labour and do anything; but man that is common and general to all men, doeth nothing. Then if he be a common man, he shall neither see, hear, perceive, nor understand, and so shall be nothing else but a very block or image.

The Church. But thou thyself shalt well perceive that he can see, hear, perceive, and work.

The People. I believe it, forsooth, that he will swallow up largely, yea, the riches of other churches. But tell me how that may be, that he may work, being a man that is common to all men?

The Church. He shall be a particular man also.

The People. Why then shall he not be one only, but he shall be two? Oh, what a fool am I, and how dull-witted! Now lo! I leave wondering. For as I hear say, as soon as he is made Pope he speaketh no more in the singular number but in the plural; so that he doth no more say, This *I* will do, or say, as they were wont in times past when they were but one man; but now he saith, *We* will do, and *we* will say, because that now he is made a double man. I am also resolved now in another doubt whereof I should never have been answered, if ye had not made me perceive it.

The Church. What doubt is that?

The People. I have heard many times say that after he is created Pope he cannot err as the Pope, but yet he may many times as a man err.

The Tragedy

THE CHURCH. That is very true.

THE PEOPLE. Now I am sure of this truth, that as he is a Pope and a common man, he cannot work anything, neither err.

THE CHURCH. Nay, as he is Pope, he worketh wonders, and cannot err because of the Holy Ghost which is assistant unto him.

THE PEOPLE. Then, by your saying, he cannot be at one time a Pope and a man, for then might he at one time err and not err. He might err as a man and not err as the Pope. Therefore at some time must he be a Pope and no man, and then can he not err. But yet can I well not perceive what monstrous beast this may be which is a Pope and no man, and again another time a man and no Pope. And I marvel wonderfully that they will rob the Popeship so much of so great a dignity, and so to leave him a bare man. Howbeit I believe indeed (although of another sort) that no Pope can err, because that Christ ever hath been, and ever shall be, the very only and true head of His Church; never shall there be any other Pope or head of Christ's Church.

THE CHURCH. I dare not affirm that our bishops can never be heretics.

THE PEOPLE. Peradventure some have been.

THE CHURCH. If any such thing chance in that he is an heretic, he ceases to be Pope. Yet is this thing true that ye must obey him and allow him

The Tragedy

so long for Pope, until he be judged and condemned for an heretic, and be deposed from his Popeship by the authority of a General Council.

THE PEOPLE. So that if he compel me to his wickedness and command me to believe his heresies before he be deposed of his Popeship, I must obey by your judgment. Surely it is handsomely counselled of you.

THE CHURCH. Thou must obey him in things right, full, and honest, and not in things that be wicked, even as ye would do if a man would force you to believe an heresy.

THE PEOPLE. Even now ye said he could not err as he was Pope; but he as Pope commandeth me to assent to his wicked opinions, and by your mind I must allow him for Pope until he be deposed by the authority of a lawful Council. Wherefore it followeth that I am bound to obey him and to be an heretic as he is.

THE CHURCH. Thou shalt not trust him in heresy and wicked doctrine, though he would command them to you a thousand times.

THE PEOPLE. And how shall I know when he favoureth and teacheth a wicked doctrine? for, by your sayings, I must believe that he cannot err, because that whatsoever he appointeth me to believe I must determine it to be wholesome doctrine and infected with no dregs of wickedness. So that in this point I shall not follow the judg-

The Tragedy

ment of mine own reason. And if I should appoint the Word of God to be judge, by your doctrine I shall not understand it but after the Pope's pleasure and exposition. And if the Pope write the Scriptures wickedly and expound them frowardly, as he is wont, and by that means frame some heresies, which he will give me, that am ignorant, to believe, shall I be bound to receive and honour them as articles of my faith? For he must be as it were my refuge and succour, and a continual guide and rule to declare Holy Scriptures. Yea, if the General Council would declare him to be a wicked man and worthy to be deposed from his office, yet ought I to allow him as Pope at the leastways until such time as he hath declared the General Council to be lawfully gathered, and that he was justly condemned in that Council. But I ask you, Is the Pope above the Council, or beneath, or equal?

THE CHURCH. Above.

THE PEOPLE. Then hath he alone more knowledge and inspiration than the whole Council. And therefore be it that the Council lawfully assembled had condemned his doctrine for heresy, yet ought I rather believe him than the whole Council, forasmuch as he is above them and more endowed with supernatural light than they be. But tell me this one thing: Ye said even now, if the Pope were an heretic, yet ought I to receive

The Tragedy

him as Pope until such time as he were deposed by the authority of a Council. Now this question I demand of you: If it should chance the Pope to be an heretic, and yet not so declared by the Council, whether were he indeed Pope or no?

THE CHURCH. If such a thing should chance, I durst not affirm him to be Pope; for then should he err indeed, and that in matters of the faith, and that as Pope. But I said even now that he could not err as Pope, although he erred as a man.

THE PEOPLE. Why then should he be no more Pope?

THE CHURCH. No, truly.

THE PEOPLE. And how or when did he lose his Popeship?

THE CHURCH. In that he is an heretic.

THE PEOPLE. If the matter be as you say, there shall be very few true Popes, no, none at all; for a man cannot be a Pope except he be an heretic; if he were in no point else, yet should he be in this, that he must believe the Pope to be the supreme head of the Church of Christ. But let us grant (although it be not so) that a man may be a Pope indeed and yet no heretic. When I am not ascertained whether he err in his mind or not, in matter that belongeth to our faith, I shall always be in a doubt whether he be the true Pope or not, and

The Tragedy

therefore shall I also be in doubt whether I shall credit his words or no, and so shall I be always doubtful in my faith.

THE CHURCH. He is always Pope although he be an heretic in his heart, if it so be that he disclose not himself to be such a one.

THE PEOPLE. What if he disclose himself to be an heretic to some other man and not to me?

THE CHURCH. Truly then should he be no more Pope.

THE PEOPLE. Then forasmuch as I know not whether he have at any time declared himself to be an heretic or not, I shall have his doctrine always in a jealousy and suspicion; neither shall I know certainly that he is Pope and cannot err, because I shall never know certainly whether he have disclosed himself to some man to be an heretic or not.

THE CHURCH. This shall be enough for thee, to think him always to be a Pope to thee so long as he hath not declared himself to thee to be an heretic. But to such as he declareth himself to be an heretic, to them he is Pope no more in very deed.

THE PEOPLE. Then if he declare himself to be an heretic to other men and not to me, he should be a Pope to me and not to others?

THE CHURCH. It is even so as ye say.

The Tragedy

THE PEOPLE. But my desire is very much to know whether he be then a Pope in himself or not. Ye cannot by any means prove him to be Pope and not Pope, and all at once. For if such a word should escape your mouth ye should perceive plainly that ye spake contradiction. Neither can ye affirm that he is Pope. For whereas he did err before others, yea, and that in the doctrine of salvation, then you must needs grant that he erreth as Pope, which thing before you said could not be. Therefore ye be forced to grant that he is not Pope. But I, which shall never have knowledge whether he hath declared to other himself to be an heretic or not, shall be in a continual doubting whether he be truly Pope or not, and so whether he can err or not, of the which thing there ariseth a certain trembling in my conscience, so that I shall never be certain and sure of the verity and truth of his doctrine. And so much the more shall I doubt, be it that he declared himself an heretic to me, because I can worse discern the true doctrine from the false, and worse judge whether his opinions be heretical or not; namely, because his word must be the first and chief rule of my faith. But let us now make an end of our disputations because the time is spent, and I must go to the Emperor, before whom I will pour out my complaints against many idle varlets, who after they perceived the greatness of our bishop they

The Tragedy

runneth to Rome in shoals, to get some offices and benefices at his hands, and few there be that bring not their trulls[1] with them, and such as do not, fall on wooing at home. But it were a heavy thing for me if Rome should be turned into Troy.

THE CHURCH. Besides this noble dignity of our bishop, I am so much occupied with an infinite number of matters, of ceremonies, of suits, and controversies, and of other profane things, that I have no time left to scratch my head. Wherefore now will I forsake you. But I will tell you one thing yet before I go. Since this man was created Pope, I have been wonderfully vexed and sick both in body and soul, even as though I had drunk a potion of poison. And I cannot tell whether I gat this sickness of too much joy wherewith I was replenished by the reason of the greatness of my promotion, or else of the intolerable burden of businesses which grow towards me daily. Now have I nothing else to say, but that I offer my new kinds of merchandise to be sold to you before others, and that better cheap than any stranger shall have them.

THE PEOPLE. I thank you for your merchant-like civility, and again I offer unto you my favour, and all my strength and power to defend and increase the greatness of your honour.

[1] *Trulls*, girls or wenches, but generally used in an opprobrious sense.

IV

THE POPE—MAN'S JUDGMENT— THE PEOPLE OF ROME

THE POPE. At the last we be come to this high honour which we have so much desired (and that is more to be wondered at) by the whole consent of all the people of Rome. I would never have thought such a number of the nobility would have come to gratify me and to increase my joy. They think verily that this our promotion shall increase and amplify their riches and power not a little. But I am informed for a certainty that many foreign churches were much vexed therewith, namely[1] such as be of the East parts. Wherefore we understand that they send ambassadors (what they be I cannot tell) to reply against the thing, and it may so be that they will drive the matter to a disputation. Now is it therefore necessary for us to arm ourselves for our defence, and, as in a matter of great weight and importance, to use a witty counsel. Wherefore, Man's Judgment (who

---

[1] *Namely*, particularly.

The Tragedy

art one of my Privy Council), with thee I think it best to consult.

MAN'S JUDGMENT. Truly, sir, I have tossed and turned all this matter in my mind again and again, and, after long and earnest fantasying, I conclude that there is no more present remedy to preserve, increase, and establish this your promotion, kingdom, and authority, than to contend and earnestly to stand in it, that it is not the ordinance of man but of God. So that it is Christ Himself who hath ordained you to be supreme head of the Church, and that with a whole fulness of power: otherwise shall ye hang always upon the Emperor, who hath placed you in this high estate of honour; and by that means as he once gave it you, so may he again take it away from you. Moreover, your empire and authority cannot be stretched out further than the coasts of the Empire of Rome extendeth; besides this, all Christendom will laugh to scorn this feigned and counterfeit dominion, crying out that Christ is the Supreme Head of His Church, and that He alone is able enough to govern it well without the help of another head or of any other deceitful man, as He hath by His ministers governed it hitherto. But if ye contend earnestly that it is Christ who hath put you in this place, ye shall both be delivered from hanging upon the Emperor, and shall also be as far above him as holy and spiritual matters are to be preferred to matters

The Tragedy

profane and worldly. So that your authority being by this means established, ye shall enter into all the coasts of the earth. There shall be no Christian men in the world, but when they shall be persuaded that Christ was the author of this ordinance (who hath made you His vicar, and of whom ye hath received this high authority) but they will come to you of their own swing[1] as though they would worship this Godhead of yours in earth, and will glory that they may obey you.

THE POPE. I would allow this counsel of you very well, if it might be brought to pass by any means that I could persuade so manifest a vanity to the world.

MAN'S JUDGMENT. The foolishness of man is grown so far now, accompanied with a wonderful deceit and wickedness, and I of myself am so subtle and crafty, that methinks it a thing easy to persuade, yea, and that I now see the means how.

THE POPE. I desire of all loves, that ye will tell me by some inkling what thing it is that ye even now mused upon; for ye may well know, that it is my joy to talk of such things.

MAN'S JUDGMENT. If there could be one jot found in the Holy Scripture whereupon we might lean for a proof that Paul the Apostle was ordered of God to be supreme and universal head of the Church Militant, yea, though it seemed writhed[2]

---

[1] *Swing*, unrestrained liberty, or natural impulse.   [2] *Writhed*, twisted.

The Tragedy

and wrasted[1] with the braakes[2] of your authority, and drawn by violence to our purpose against the natural sense, and yet so that there were some likelihood therein, the victory were ours. For it is evident by the Word of God that Paul was some time at Rome, and though he were then in prison, yet shall we persuade by all means possible that he was made bishop of this city, whose office and dignity you have by inheritance and succession obtained. I have occupied my fantasy to and fro, and have chewed this question diligently, and so at the last I perceive that there be many words in the Holy Scripture which with a little wresting would make the blind, ignorant, common people give credit to this vain opinion, that Paul was the chief of all the apostles and universal head of all the Churches of Christ. And yet shall we not therefore obtain all our purpose. For the self-same Holy Scripture is in other places directly and in plain words against us. Forasmuch as it is evident that Paul the Apostle was none of the twelve apostles of Christ ; yea, and when Christ was here in earth, he was His enemy and persecutor, and afterward also a certain space. Neither is it likely that Christ would ascend into Heaven, but would first well foresee to His Church, and leave unto it one certain head to be His vicar and occupy His room. This thing was very necessary for Him

[1] *Wrasted*, torn.   [2] *Braakes*, brambles.

The Tragedy

to do. This last reason must we allege earnestly and defend it stoutly, if we intend to obtain our purpose. But now have I devised a far better way. There be many places in the Gospel which may easily be writhed[1] to our purpose; that is to say, whereby some likelihood may be alleged that Peter the Apostle was pronounced chief of the apostles by Christ's own mouth, and was created supreme head of His Church Militant. Now if we could bring him to Rome, and make him bishop of this city, it shall be an easy thing to persuade that you be his successor, and so shall we obtain all our purpose.

THE POPE. Will ye attempt to bring Peter now to Rome, and he died so many years agone? This thing methinketh cannot be.

MAN'S JUDGMENT. In case I should raise him up from death and bring him to Rome, and so in conclusion make him bishop of this city, what would ye say?

THE POPE. Marry! I would withstand it with tooth and nail. Neither canst thou make him bishop of this city, but thou shalt bereave me of this my dignity.

MAN'S JUDGMENT. If I should make him bishop, and yet rob you not of your honour, but rather establish you and make you his successor, should it not please you?

[1] *Writhed*, twisted.

The Tragedy

THE POPE. Yes, wonderfully. But I see not how that may be brought about.

MAN'S JUDGMENT. I have written certain epistles in the name of those Christian men which were at Rome in the time of the beginning of the Church, wherein there is often mention made of Peter as though he had been at Rome, and not only bishop of this city, but also Pope, and universal head of all the Church Militant, as though sundry constitutions had been then by him made. And because ye shall praise my wit the more, I wrote all this gear in so wonderful old books, that for age they could scarcely hang together. There is no man that seeth them but they will judge they were written a thousand years agone and more. Let us make the people believe that these books be newly found by chance in some old rotten library, and so when this rumour shall once be blown abroad, the common people will straight believe that Peter was at Rome; if there were no other cause, yet that he came for religion's sake, on pilgrimage to saints' relics, and to receive the jubilee and full pardon.

THE POPE. Yet is not all this enough. For be it that he were at Rome, that, notwithstanding, he departed after he had received the jubilee, and took his popeship away with him, and so shall we be no longer his successors. Therefore is it needful that as ye have brought him to Rome, so ye cause him also to die at Rome.

The Tragedy

MAN'S JUDGMENT. Abide a while. This is the thing I went about; I have done this thing already. And for a confirmation of the whole matter I got me an old foul bone of a dead carcase, into the which I did put a paper which had these words contained in it :—This is the head of Saint Peter the first Pope of Rome. Moreover I have compassed this head about with another head of silver, and have so framed it with a great beard, that it appeareth verily to be Saint Peter's head. And I doubt not but that this feigned matter may be easily persuaded to the people, if it be published abroad by your authority.

THE POPE. We must of necessity grant that Peter was crucified upon a cross, for so did Christ prophesy of him. Now it is well known that it was the use of the Jews, and not of the Romans, to hang men upon the cross. Wherefore I see not how the people will believe that Peter was killed at Rome and put upon the cross by the Romans. _{John xxi.}

MAN'S JUDGMENT. Tush! Men will not be so curious in other men's matters to search every point of them so narrowly. And again, we shall have a sure staff to lean to, whereunto we may always resort. We will say that God would have it so that Christ's words might be fulfilled. Who can prove the contrary? Besides this, I have many remedies and means how to preserve, increase, and establish you in this high honour, as ye

The Tragedy

shall see by experience; neither will I let any good occasion overslip that may be to your furtherance. Be it that there come ambassadors to the city of Rome: I alone will answer them all as they ought to be answered. In the mean space shall you begin a little and little to publish abroad that it is Christ who hath made you Pope, and that ye be the successor of Peter, the high Bishop of Rome.

THE POPE. But what will then the Emperor say, when he shall perceive that we noise it abroad that it was Christ, and not he, which made me Pope?

MAN'S JUDGMENT. Our answer shall be that ye were declared and confirmed the chief bishop by the Emperor's Majesty, but yet that it was Christ who hath placed you in so high a seat, even as He did your predecessors before you. But lo! one whom ye saw not, a gentleman called the People of Rome. [*Enter the* PEOPLE OF ROME.] I think he cometh to see you and to do his duty. I pray you, offer him your foot to kiss that ye may so begin to bring that thing into a laudable custom.

THE POPE.[1] And even for the same very purpose have I caused a red cross to be made on the over part of my foot.

---

[1] In the text this speech is put into the mouth of the *People*; but it is obviously the *Pope* who is intended, and there has been an error in transcribing or printing.

The Tragedy

MAN'S JUDGMENT. Although many think that to be done of you in despite of the cross, yet is it justly and well done to set the cross in the lowest place, yea, and Christ Himself also, that your glory may be announced to a most high state. Namely, for that we know the cross of Christ always to be hated of the wise men of this world. And to say the truth, it had been more meet for you to have caused the cross to be set under the sole of your foot, if it had not been painful for you to lift up your foot so oft to all such as would kiss it. But I will withdraw myself for a time, that you may commune alone at your pleasure with this son of yours. [*Exit.*]

THE PEOPLE. Oh, happy and blessed am I, since I have thus much favour showed me, that I may be suffered to come and kiss these holy and blessed feet.

THE POPE. In consideration that this benefit may be the more esteemed, we grant you out of the treasures of Peter and Paul and other holy apostles and saints forty times' forty days of pardon.

THE PEOPLE. A goodly reward, and we thank you highly; we thank you, I say, as speaking to many which be most holy and most blessed Popes.

THE POPE. What meanest thou by that—that thou didst call us most blessed and most holy Popes in the plural number? Thinkest thou

The Tragedy

that we be many Popes? Seest thou not us only placed in this dignity?

THE PEOPLE. Pardon thou me, I beseech thee, most holy and blessed Father. When I heard thee speak in the plural number I thought that there had been two Popes at the least.

THE POPE. Dost thou not perceive thyself to speak unreverently? Thou sayest, pardon thou me. Understandest thou not that thou shouldest of nurture and due reverence speak to us in the plural number? And that because He worketh continually in us who first advanced us to this high dignity, for we be not alone in working. Otherwise when thou shouldest speak by name to us, thou oughtest to speak in the singular number, and that because our person and dignity is but one.

THE PEOPLE. I beseech your Holiness to pardon me, because I am not yet acquainted with these kinds of ceremonies. Ye have heard, I think, of the number of ambassadors which be sent from sundry parts of the world, of whom a great company be come to Rome already.

THE POPE. For what purpose say they that they be come?

THE PEOPLE. To reply against you, being offended with this high honour that the Emperor hath given you.

THE POPE. We have received this Popeship of Christ, and not of the Emperor.

The Tragedy

THE PEOPLE. Truly I heard say it was given of the Emperor.

THE POPE. And who told thee so?

THE PEOPLE. Your Church of Rome, of whom I have perceived of late in communication that it was given you of Cæsar's Majesty.

THE POPE. As concerning this matter, she is not advised what she saith.

THE PEOPLE. And she saith plainly that she cannot err.

THE POPE. Truth, indeed, no more can she when she is informed and instructed of me. Ye know right well, according to the doctrine of Paul, that a woman must be subject to her husband, and so far forth she speaketh well, as she receiveth knowledge of him. Of the same fashion the Church of Rome speaketh well and erreth not, so far forth as she receiveth instructions and knowledge of me; for she is my spouse, and therefore is she my wife.

THE PEOPLE. Why, how then? Doth she not acknowledge Christ to be her spouse?

THE POPE. Yes, truly, she is both Christ's spouse and mine.

THE PEOPLE. This is the first time that ever I heard that one woman may have two husbands. I have heard of sundry men that hath had many wives; but I never heard of one woman that hath had many husbands. But let this pass, and let us return again to our former talk. And most

[marginal note: 1 Cor. vii. and xi., Ephes. v.]

The Tragedy

humbly this one thing I beseech your Holiness it will vouchsafe to tell me : How hath your Holiness obtained this high bishopric at Christ's hand ?

THE POPE. We will tell thee. Christ, being the head of the Church, ordained Peter, before He ascended into Heaven, to be His vicar and successor. And because he came to Rome and brought his high Popeship with him, and dying there hath left the same to his successors, that is to say, the other Bishops of Rome in order, we now, being Bishop of Rome, have received of Christ by succession and inheritance this high pontifical dignity, power, and authority.

THE PEOPLE. I hear news now that I never heard before, namely this, that Peter was ever at Rome. I am of an exceeding great age (as ye see) and have dwelt in Rome in Peter's days. And so desireful I was to hear news, that if ever he had come to Rome no doubt I would have seen him ; and it had been for none other cause, yet truly would I so have done for his worthy name's sake, wherewith he filled our city ; neither would I have suffered the remembrance of him to have decayed, even as I have diligently preserved until this day fresh the remembrance of Paul. No man can either think or show what time he was here and I absent. For I never went out of this city.

THE POPE. All the time whilst he was here,

The Tragedy

for the most part he was in prison, and therefore is it no marvel though thou sawest him not.

THE PEOPLE. I have been always, and am till this day, exceeding quisitive[1] and curious in searching of news. My study is to know what is done everywhere; I range and wander even to the very prisons. It is not possible that such a man should at any time have come to Rome and have been cast in prison for the Gospel's sake, but I should have heard of it. Howbeit I not only never saw him, but moreover I never heard of any man living that ever he was at Rome, saving even now of your Holiness.

THE POPE. It may so be that whiles he was at Rome he lay hid in some corner.

THE PEOPLE. How then preached he the Gospel here, by the occasion whereof he was cast in prison, and at the last hanged upon the cross? Besides this, if he were Bishop of Rome, how was he chosen to that dignity if he were not known whiles he remained in Rome?

THE POPE. Mark well this thing that I shall say unto thee. Thou must be circumspect and wise when it shall chance thee to reason of this matter. For the day may come when we shall call thee forth to be a witness in it. Which thing, if it happen, we will thee to say that thou diddest both see and know him.

[1] *Quisitive*, inquisitive.

The Tragedy

THE PEOPLE. What! would ye have me lie lustily and so sensibly that every man might perceive it?

THE POPE. We absolve thee of this fault, and further, we let thee to wit that we do all these things of a good and holy intent, and for the glory of God. And this dare we be bold to say, that great honour and profit shall arise to thee by the increasing of our dignity.

THE PEOPLE. If I be absolved of this lie, I cannot but do for you in all other things, because that heresy shall ensue to me a very great commodity; but lest I should be taken with my lie I would fain know what I shall answer when I am asked, namely of the time when Peter was at Rome.

THE POPE. Thou shalt say that he dwelled at Rome still, after he came once thither, until his dying day.

THE PEOPLE. Being demanded when he came first, shall I say before Paul or after?

THE POPE. It is best for thee to say before Paul, lest men should have occasion to think that Paul was Bishop of Rome before Peter.

THE PEOPLE. Now call I to remembrance when Paul's cause was first heard here at Rome before Cæsar's throne, all Christian men forsook him, as he himself writeth in a certain epistle he made to Timothy. Wherefore it must then be granted that he was then forsaken of Peter for

2 Timothy iv.

The Tragedy

fear. Which thing seemeth not likely that there should so great a fault be found in Peter, who had so earnest and fervent a zeal towards religion, and full of Christian charity, namely[1] after Christ ascended into Heaven and replenished him with the Holy Ghost.

THE POPE. I could not remember so hard a doubt as this is. It is best, then, to say that Peter came when Paul was already examined.

THE PEOPLE. Again being demanded whether he were chosen Bishop of Rome in this city or not, what answer shall I make?

THE POPE. Marry! thou shalt constantly say yea.

THE PEOPLE. Well, then received he his bishopric of men, and not simply and only of Christ. How then shall it be true that he was pronounced by Christ head of all other churches?

THE POPE. Thou understandest not this matter. Peter had two bishoprics, one particular and another general. The chief, that is to say, the general, he received of Christ, whereby he is bishop and head of all other churches and bishoprics. The former, that is to say, the particular, he received of men, whereby he was the Bishop of Rome.

THE PEOPLE. I have seen amongst them which profess monkery when they go on their general

---

[1] *Namely*, particularly.

The Tragedy

visitations of the provinces committed to their charge, they will not be so General Provincials that they will take upon them to remove them away whom they find, but suffer them to remain and do their office as they did before, and they also be contented with their office of visitation. Of a like sort methinketh if Christ had ordained Peter a universal bishop of all other bishops, his duty should be to visit all other churches, and yet to leave every bishop remaining in his own diocese, and he himself to be contented with his own office, and regard nothing to be created bishop of every sundry church. But I pray you this one thing : Was Peter a bishop before he was made Bishop of Rome and Antioch, or not?

THE POPE. He was but yet a general bishop of the whole Church of Christ, and no several Bishop of Rome or Antioch.

THE PEOPLE. Then was he called an universal bishop of Christ and of His Church, by the means whereof he was called a Christian bishop and not the Bishop of Rome.

THE POPE. It is very true as ye say.

THE PEOPLE. Now marvel I very much why, after he was made Bishop of Rome, he refused the first title, and received the latter, seeing that his last bishopric was no cause why he should lose the first ; that notwithstanding he would no more be called the Chief Christian Bishop but the Bishop

The Tragedy

of Rome. And yet without controversy the first title is more worthy title than is the latter. And as for the first name and title, he had it of Christ, the latter of man. If Peter at any time would have received and allowed to be called the Chief Christian Bishop, surely your predecessors would have usurped and challenged the same title. Which thing, because it is not done, but they be called the Bishops of Rome, many men will think that neither they, neither any of their predecessors, were ever universal bishop of all churches. For if that had so been, truly they would have changed the particular title with the more general and more worthy title, or at the leastways your Holiness should now at the last begin to be called, neither the chief, neither the Romish bishop, but a Christian bishop of Christ and of His congregation, and create some private Bishop of Rome in your stead.

The Pope. Ye cannot persuade us to be so much a fool that we will refuse the bishopric of Rome to run in visitation of churches hither and thither like Egyptians. We will hold fast this bishopric of Rome, and furthermore we will be, and require so to be, accounted the supreme head of all other bishops.

The People. As for my part, I am right well contented and satisfied howsoever the matter go ; neither did I move this matter for any other

The Tragedy

purpose, but because that name and title of a Christian bishop seemeth to me much more excellent than to be called Bishop of Rome. But, and it may like your Holiness, was Peter the first Bishop of Rome?

THE POPE. That is without question.

THE PEOPLE. Surely I marvel much that Paul was so notable an apostle, and so much esteemed before Peter, and yet was not made Bishop of Rome. And another thing I marvel at much more, that although the Church of Christ was at Rome, yea, and that many years before Paul came thither, and many wise and godly men were in it (as it appeareth in the epistle which Paul wrote especially to them, where he saluteth them by name), yet that their church was so evil ordered that it lacked a bishop.

THE POPE. There were bishops there; but Peter was not the first Bishop of Rome, but the first chief bishop of all other, and he made an ordinance that all Bishops of Rome which should afterwards follow him should also be the highest bishops above all other.

THE PEOPLE. Verily I cannot see from whence Peter had this authority to make such an ordinance, that all Bishops of Rome should be Popes and vicars of Christ, although they were wicked hellhounds. Methinketh it had been done according to justice and equity, if any should be ordained

The Tragedy

bishop above all other bishops and churches, the same should be chosen by the consent of all bishops and all churches. And this thing is most of all to be marvelled at, how it may come to pass that all your predecessors, from Peter even until this day, were highest bishops and head of all churches, and yet used not they this authority. No, there was never communication of it before this present.

THE POPE. Never think that that is so, as though they were not chief bishops in very deed; but it was not needful for them to use their authority; and of a certain modesty they declared not themselves chief bishops as they were. But now there be so many heresies arisen in the Church of God, such sundry sects and dissensions, that we have thought it necessary for a remedy against so many mischiefs, to declare ourselves, what we have by Christ, and so to use our most high authority.

THE PEOPLE. I understand you well, namely because the Chief Bishops of Rome (as I hear say) cannot err. This one thing also cannot I hide, which seemeth to me somewhat. If they have received this high authority of Christ, they ought by no means to keep it secret and hid, but to disclose it to the whole world, whether they used it or not, according as the circumstances of things, pardons, times, and places should require; and

The Tragedy

that should the more diligently have been done, for that it is now opened with a great offence of all good and godly men ; and the worst point of all is that men be not so foolish nowadays that they will give any credit unto you. But I, as a good child of your Holiness, will always show myself obedient, and ready to believe you. And because I would trouble your Holiness no longer, with your blessed license I will depart.

V

THOMAS MASSUCCIUS, THE MASTER OF THE HORSE — LEPIDUS, THE POPE'S CHAMBERLAIN

MASSUCCIUS. Yonder I see Master Lepidus coming hastily and cheerfully out of the Emperor's court. I will wait upon him to know whether he bring us any good tidings. God save you, Master Lepidus! Surely you bring us some good news, as a man would judge by your countenance, ye seem so pleasant and merry.

LEPIDUS. I have so much joy trussed up in this breast of mine that I can scarcely stay myself within my skin.

MASSUCCIUS. As noble hearts of the world may be esteemed so much the more happy the larger they spread abroad their happy state and felicity, wherefore I beseech you vouchsafe to tell me whereof this joy of yours ariseth, that your joy may be increased even with the telling thereof.

LEPIDUS. Why, is it your chance alone not

The Tragedy

to hear of the disputation that hath been in the court of Rome, and of that triumph and victory that we have obtained?

MASSUCCIUS. I know nothing else but that the last day I heard tell of certain ambassadors which came from sundry coasts of the world to Rome, which would reply with open mouth against this high authority of the Pope.

LEPIDUS. This day was there an open and solemn disputation in the presence of Cæsar's Majesty of this matter, and in conclusion our men have obtained the high power of the Pope.

MASSUCCIUS. I would fain know what reasons they had to bring this unworthy matter to pass.

LEPIDUS. Surely I know a great number of them, and some of them were such that I dare not disclose them unto you, unless ye promise me before to keep them to yourself.

MASSUCCIUS. If they be such reasons as may not be lawfully kept secret, ye require in vain to keep counsel of them, and though I swear a thousand times, yet ought I not to keep it; but if I may lawfully and ought to keep it secret, ye may have so much credit in me that ye may believe I will keep counsel without an oath. If ye think me a man not worthy to be trusted, then are ye the more to blame to require an oath of me, from the which the Pope may easily absolve me by reason of the high power that he now hath.

The Tragedy

Howbeit I promise you by the faith of a Christian man to keep counsel if I may do it lawfully.

LEPIDUS. Forasmuch as I trust you not a little by the reason of our old friendship, I cannot but disclose the whole matter unto you. When the Holiness of our lord and master heard say that the most part of the whole world was much troubled for this wonderful dignity whereunto he hath attained, and that also their ambassadors were come to cry out against it openly, he took these ways first which appeared to make very much for his purpose. As soon as they came to Rome he sent unto them secretly goodly flagons of the best wine that could be got of Malmsey, of wine of Tribiana, of St. John, of Greece, and of Corsica.

MASSUCCIUS. Surely this was a goodly beginning that he made to the strangers whereby to compass and overcome them, and (as it were) to clasp them by the very throat.

LEPIDUS. He sent moreover a goodly present and a beautiful[1] of blessings, pardons, jubilees, privileges, immunities, and very rich promises of benefits, and of all other such gifts which either he now had or else should have hereafter. After this he sent unto every one of them clean remission *a poena et culpa*. Then he absolved them of

---

[1] *Beautiful*, used here as a noun. In the sixteenth century it was no uncommon thing to use adjectives as nouns. Thus in *Henry VI*. Shakspere speaks of "the *silent* of the night," and in *The Tempest* of "the *vast* of night."

The Tragedy

their oaths that they had made to such as had sent them.

MASSUCCIUS. Very well; that by the means thereof he might the more easily corrupt them.

LEPIDUS. Nay, that they, being absolved and set free from their oaths, might more easily and freely stick to the truth. And so he caused his servants to say unto them, lest peradventure men should conceive some evil opinion of them. He signified also unto them that he was very joyful when he heard of their coming to Rome that they might see with their own eyes and judge with their own knowledge, and know the whole truth of the matter, even as it was, so that at their return home again into their countries they might shine to orber[1] with the light of their knowledge who peradventure should otherwise remain in the darkness of ignorance or of some false surmise.

MASSUCCIUS. And if he were not Pope I durst be bold to say he lied shamefully in so saying. For I am sure that the coming of the ambassadors was as pleasant to him as though one had hurled salt into his eyes.

LEPIDUS. And because the disputation of his pontifical prerogative must be in the presence of Cæsar, and the Pope's holiness for sundry con-

---

[1] *Orber*, literally to make round, but probably used here in a metaphorical sense, *i.e.* to perfect or complete, a sphere being considered the most perfect form.

The Tragedy

siderations would defend it to be of God, and given to him by Christ and not by the Emperor, he, fearing lest by this means the Emperor's Majesty would be vexed, signified unto him that he would propound and establish the matter after this sort; not because he did not acknowledge that he had this dignity only of him, at whose commandment he would always be, and recognise him to be his singular patron and defender, but because he would deliver him from all suspicion and slander, which many without cloaking did object, as though it were very evil done of him which bestowed this honour upon one mortal man; and lest also other princes, taking example of him, would likewise establish in their dominions sundry supreme heads, and that should breed schisms and dissensions in the Church of Christ.

MASSUCCIUS. Oh, what an ass-head was he, if ever he would assent hereunto!

LEPIDUS. Assent! Yea, and praise him also, even as though it had been a thing devised by God Himself, and sent to him from God. When they came to the very disputation, the Emperor had a plentiful oration, wherein he exhorted them all that came thither to entreat upon that matter, to peace, concord and unity, and when it came to the Pope's course to speak, because he would keep his state, he commanded Master Hypocrite to speak in his name, and he so handled himself with

The Tragedy

counterfeit words and gesture, and went about with such a force of eloquence to persuade them that the Pope's Holiness was not moved of himself to accept so high a state, but rather earnestly withstood it, and yet having an eye to the glory of God, and following the moving of the Holy Ghost, at length he took this heavy and sharp cross of the Popeship upon him ; this, I say, he persuaded in such sort that he almost made me believe it was true, as he said. And so I myself did many times assent to him in that he said, that if he could with a safe conscience leave this high authority he both readily and gladly would so do. But that might not be, because by that means he should do God great injury. But seeing the matter was so, he was right glad that there was at this present a disputation appointed of so great and weighty a matter, whereby the truth thereof might be known to all men. And thus at last began the disputation :—Where first arose the Ambassador of Constantinople, a very wise man, and with a loud voice said before the great audience there assembled ; That all the churches of the universal world were highly offended with this wonderful and wicked primacy of the Bishop of Rome, which never was heard of before. And that Christ Himself was the true and only Head of His Church in this militant exile ; even as He is also the Head of the triumphant Church of the Heavenly Jerusalem,

The Ambassador of Constantinople, his reasons.

The Tragedy

and that He never ordained any other head. Wherefore it was to be thought that this wicked innovation was not of God, and in case it were ordained of God, yet could not this supreme honour belong to the Bishop of Rome. Therefore was it not only a device of man, but wicked also, and wrongful, and therefore altogether devilish, and not to be suffered. Not a thing ordained of God, as all might perceive that have any judgment; and so false it was that there could be any one word found in all Scripture for the defence of this primacy, that there be a number of sayings directly against it. Then arose Master Falsidicus, and interrupting the Ambassador in his matter, spake after this sort for the Pope's defence :—Nay, in Holy Scripture there is not one word contrary, but many things be there which make for it. First and foremost ye know right well that Christ said to Peter, Thou art Peter, and upon this rock will I build my Church. Now if Peter were made the true and only foundation, not of this or that particular church, but of the whole universal Church of Christ, by the assent and appointment of Christ, it must of force be granted that the Church was sustained and governed by Peter, whilst he lived here in earth, and so was he the universal head of the Church, as after him Peter's successors were and be the true heads of the Church. Hereunto the Ambassador made answer :—If ye fall a-jesting

The Tragedy

in an earnest manner, it is not to be commended in matters of importance. But if ye speak as ye think, I marvel much that ye be ignorant. Is it possible ye should be in such an heresy to think Peter was the head and foundation of the Church of Christ, that is to say of all the faithful? Truly if it were so, the Church of Christ in times past should have had a very feeble and weak foundation, and many times should it have fallen by reason of the feebleness of so slender a ground. And again, it is an extreme weakness and plain idolatry to attribute that to Peter, which appertaineth only to Christ. Christ is only that proved corner, excellent, sure and stable stone, which according to
<small>Dan. ii.</small> the prophecy of Daniel shall break all the kingdoms of the world, and itself shall endure forever a stable and strong foundation of the kingdom and congregation of Christ, which thing is confirmed,
<small>Esay xxviii.</small> not only by the testimony of Daniel, but of Esay
<small>Psalm cxviii. Matt. xxi. Ephes. ii.</small> also, and of David, and by the authority of Christ Himself. And Paul the Apostle teacheth the very same doctrine, when he saith that we must be raised up in this holy building of the Church, not upon Peter but upon Christ, the most strong foundation of the prophets and of the apostles.
<small>1 Peter ii.</small> The selfsame doctrine is established and confirmed by the witness of Peter. And that because a number of light fellows might chance to stumble at this stone, inasmuch that they should think

The Tragedy

Christ, during the time of His being in earth, was the foundation of His Church, but when He was once lifted up into Heaven, He left Peter in His stead, Paul the Apostle and most faithful interpreter of God's heavenly will teacheth the contrary in special words, when he saith : There can none other foundation be laid for the Church of Christ besides that is already laid, that is to say, Christ. And if Christ must always be the true and only foundation of His Church, it must needs be confessed, that never was, or else ever shall be, any other foundation of the Church of Christ, and therefore none other true and universal Head. Now when Peter had professed the very true confession of Christ that He was the Son of God, and Christ had said to him, Thou art Peter, and upon this rock I will build my Church, he showed and declared himself to be the lively rock and strong foundation of His Church, by the means whereof he began to be called Peter, whereas before he was called Simon ; and all was by the reason of his confession, and of the revelation of the Heavenly Father that he cleaved by faith to Christ, the strongest rock and foundation of His Church. The selfsame thing happened to all those that believe truly in Christ which happened to Peter. For they are blessed and have everlasting life, as Christ Himself doth witness, and they may be called Peters, because by the help of

Margin notes: 1 Cor. iii. b. Matt. i. vi. c. Matt. i. vi. c. Mark viii. d. Luke ix. c. John vi. g. 1 Cor. x. a.

The Tragedy

lively faith they cleave to the lively and unchangeable rock which is Christ, even as Christian men have their name of Christ, and against them that believe of such a sort, the very gates of Hell shall not prevail. Where it is to be noted that gates were wont to be exceeding strong, and surely defended, in the which gates judgment in times past was wont to be exercised; and therefore when our Saviour Christ nameth the gates of Hell, He understandeth the power and wisdom of His adversaries, or else truly He understandeth sin, whereby, as it were by gates, men enter into Hell; as though He had said, all the power, subtlety, false doctrine, threatenings and flatterings of the world, furnished with their Hell and Paradise, shall not prevail against His Church: and that Christ by this rock, whereupon He said He would build His Church, did understand and mean Himself. St. Austen[1] doth write in an homily which he hath written upon this place, where he saith, If Christ would have laid the foundation of His Church upon Peter, truly He would have said: Thou art Peter, and upon thee will I build my Church. Although Chrysostom and Theophilact do expound this place as though Christ would have the sound profession and sound faith in Christ to be understanded by this word rock. Which faith may be called until this day the foundation of the Church of Christ, forasmuch

[1] St. Augustine.

The Tragedy

as the congregation of the chosen cleaveth to Christ, the chief and true foundation of this Church by faith. Now then because Christ is always the true and only foundation of His Church, and also that faith is the thing whereby we be joined to Christ, one must of necessity grant that it is as false as God is true that some men say : That Peter or some other Bishop of Rome is the foundation of the Church of Christendom. Paul, writing to the Galatians, saith not that Peter was the foundation of the Church of Christ, but called him a pillar, as he calleth also James and John, making him equal, but not superior. If there were ever any man that said, that Christ laid the foundation of His Church upon Peter, if they were of right judgments, they minded to declare nothing else but that it was builded upon the faith of Christ, which faith the chosen and elect have, even as Peter had.

Galatians ii. *b*.

MASSUCCIUS. But my belief was always that Christ was the only One who ruled, governed, and sustained His Church, neither can I persuade to myself the contrary. But that same Master Falsidicus, as far as I perceive, doth fantasy that Christ governed and sustained His Church for a season, and afterward intending to ascend into Heaven, because He could not be at the selfsame time in Heaven, and also sustain and govern His congregation, as though it had been one tired with ruling and labouring, left Peter in His place, and so after

The Tragedy

them all the Bishops of Rome in ordinary succession. Howbeit, if men and not Christ were the foundation of the Church of Christendom which did sustain and bear the same, truly it should have weak and very feeble pillars to lean upon, and so feeble that it would not once, but more than a thousand times, have been overthrown, namely[1] because this thing is without controversy :—When the Bishop of Rome is dead, there is not by and by another chosen in his room, but some days at the least come between, wherein the Church of Christ should lack a head, though it never lacked one at any time else. Now may you perceive whether the Church were then destroyed or not. And this dare I boldly say, if the Church should lean upon men after this sort, as upon the foundation, Hell gates had prevailed against it long before this time. Furthermore, if we were grounded upon men and should trust to them as to our groundwork and foundation, we should be all accursed according to the saying : Cursed be that man which putteth his trust in man. And then should not our Church be the Church of Christ, but the synagogue of Satan, and Peter should have erred exceedingly, Christ being lifted up into the high place of Heaven, and he left for the foundation of the Church in earth, in that he exhorteth Christian men not to build upon him, but upon Christ, the true and sure

Jere. ii.

[1] *Namely*, particularly.

The Tragedy

foundation and groundwork of His Church. And this also is very true: even as Christ did not only ask Peter, but all the rest of the apostles with him, when He said: But whom say ye that I am? so also Peter made answer in the name of all the apostles, or else they all being demanded should every one have answered for themselves. But there was much communication amongst them at sundry times before, as they all confessed with one accord that He was the Son of God, although Judas with a lively¹ faith believed not so. And Christ at another time asked all His apostles: Will you also depart? Peter only in the name of the rest made answer: Thou hast the words of eternal life. Which thing is evident of the words that follow: To whom shall we go; we knew and believed long agone that Thou art Christ the very Son of the living God. Of a like sort he answereth in the name of them all, when he spake these words: Thou art Christ the Son of God. And because Peter in the name of them all confessed Christ to be the Son of God, ye must grant that when Christ said, Thou art Peter, and upon this rock will I build my Church, that He spake not only to Peter, but to them all, although it were in the name of Peter. As though He had said: Peter only is not the lively rock, but all such as follow- [Matt. xvi. c.] [Mark viii. d.] [Luke ix. c.] [John vi. g.] [John vi.] [1 Cor. x.] [Matt. xxi.]

¹ *Lively faith*, so in the text, but probably a typographical error for 'lively *want* of faith.'

The Tragedy

ing his example verily believe and confess Christ to be the Son of God, be lively rocks which He builded upon the unchangeable and precious cornerstone, Christ the only foundation of His Church. But, I pray you, what said Master Falsidicus to such things as were objected?

LEPIDUS. Would ye know, said he, how Christ minded by these words to make Peter the foundation and head of His Church? Read the words that follow, and ye shall perceive that He spake to Peter when He said, To thee will I give the keys of the kingdom of Heaven. And whatsoever thou shalt bind in earth it shall also be bound in Heaven, and whatsoever thou loosest in earth it shall be loosed in Heaven. It is not to be thought but that Christ, being most true of His promise, performed most abundantly that whatsoever He promised to Peter. And so must it be granted, that the keys of the kingdom of Heaven were delivered to Peter, and therefore hath he power to open and to shut up Heaven to whomsoever it shall please him, and to bring in and drive out whom he shall think meet, as he will himself; so may he loose also and bind. And forasmuch as by the words of Christ, Peter only had the authority to loose and bind, to open and shut up Heaven, it followeth that Christ gave authority full and whole to Peter, and ordained him only to be head of His Church.

MASSUCCIUS. If only Peter and the Bishops of

The Tragedy

Rome have the keys of the kingdom of Heaven, and they only have power to open the same, forsooth I would not die when the see of Rome is vacant and void of a bishop. For then should there be nobody which should open Heaven gates to me. And I marvel, moreover, of whom they got the keys of Purgatory, for it appeareth by their own confession, that Christ gave him none other keys but of the kingdom of Heaven only. But I could have choked him, even with one word.

LEPIDUS. How?

MASSUCCIUS. Thus would I have said: The Emperor's porter hath the key of the Emperor's court and hath authority to open and shut, and the mayor of a city hath authority to bind and loose, and yet neither of them both is the Emperor. Of a like sort, be it that Peter had the keys and authority to bind and loose, it followeth not therefore that he is the head and lord of the Church of God, that he is equal with Christ, or else at least His vicar of equal authority by whom our faith may be stable and sure, that he is the umpire and judge of all controversies which arise in Holy Scripture. But tell me this one thing: what answer made the Ambassador of Constantinople to this thing?

LEPIDUS. First he answered that Christ gave not the keys even then to Peter, but promised them only, not doubting but that Christ kept promise with him. But he was desirous to know

The Tragedy

of Master Falsidicus the time when He delivered the keys to Peter, and gave him authority to loose and to bind, and what words He said when He gave them. For by that means the truth might appear what was meant by these keys, and what is this authority. To this Master Falsidicus made answer, that He assured Peter of them when after His resurrection He asked Peter whether he loved Him more earnestly than the rest did or not. Unto whom Peter made answer saying, Thou knowest, O Lord, that I love Thee. Then Christ gave him injunctions to feed His sheep. In the very self-same hour He made him the chief shepherd and bishop of all souls.

Then the Ambassador of Constantinople, smiling, said : If preaching the word of God be the feeding of souls (as the holy doctors with one assent doth expound it), it is without doubt that that office was not only given to Peter, but also to all the rest of the apostles, and namely[1] to Paul, who writeth in special words, that he laboured more than all the rest did in the ministry of preaching. Yea, and Christ Himself, before He spake these words to Peter, commanded the selfsame thing to all the apostles, saying, Go ye throughout the universal world, and preach the Gospel to all creatures. So that it cannot be said that the office of preaching was given by Christ only to Peter and to the

[1] *Namely*, particularly.

The Tragedy

Bishops of Rome in ordinary succession after him, by whose appointment it should also descend to other. For then must it be granted that there hath been very few lawful and true bishops which had lawful authority to preach, and so few that Peter only may be accounted the true bishop which preached lawfully, and a few besides, who were by him appointed in such countries whereat he preached. By this means Paul and the eleven apostles, and such as were by them converted to the faith, neither were truly bishops, neither yet preached lawfully, because they neither had their bishopric, neither authority to preach of Peter. And moreover, none after the death of Peter should have been made bishop, neither have licence to preach besides the Bishop of Rome. And truly the Bishops of Rome have committed a grievous offence in that they have hid this large and great authority of theirs that they had so necessary in the Church of God.

Then replied Master Falsidicus, Even as Peter (quoth he) loved Christ more earnestly than the rest of the apostles, as it is plain by the words of his answer, when Christ demanded him whether he loved Him more fervently than the rest did : so had he more authority given unto him over the sheep of Christ than the rest of the apostles. To this answered the Ambassador of Constantinople—

And where, I pray you, have you found that Peter's answer was to Christ, that He was more

The Tragedy

earnestly beloved of him than of the rest of the apostles? Notwithstanding that he was so demanded, yet his answer was only in this wise, Thou knowest, O Lord, that Thou art beloved of me. He said not, Thou knowest, O Lord, that Thou art more fervently beloved of me than of the rest. For so could he never have said without great arrogancy, because it was unknown to him how much the rest loved Christ. But let it be granted that Christ was more earnestly beloved of Peter than of the rest, doth it therefore follow that Christ gave him more power? Or in case He gave him more, was it therefore most of all? For it is not all one thing to say, Feed my sheep, and to say, Be thou head of my Church, or else, Take thou more authority than the other apostles. And as for that Christ demanded of him this, whether he loved Him or not, it was done for this end and purpose, that his love being declared by this confessing might countervail¹ and somewhat make amends for his fault. When he thrice denied Him, He minded to have Peter's love sealed (as it were), and warranted, before He would commit unto him the cure of souls, that all men might know no man can be a good shepherd unless he love Christ earnestly. Furthermore, if your reason were a good reason, it should rather follow thereof that Christ declared John the chief bishop than Peter. For

¹ *Countervail*, to counteract or compensate.

The Tragedy

it is written of John, This is the disciple whom Christ loved. Wherefore if he were beloved of Christ above other, He gave unto him more worthy gifts, and replenished him more abundantly with grace, and therefore placed him above the other, and namely for that he was more meet for the purpose, by the reason of the excellent gifts which he received at God's hands. And so much the more, because it should rather appear that John loved Christ more than the other did, and was loved again of Christ, and knew Him more thoroughly, and therefore more like to be judged worthy to feed the sheep of Christ. It may be proved that Christ would have ordained him the universal shepherd, not only by reason of the noble light of the heavenly spirit, wherewith he was endued, and was always nigh and familiar to Christ, and amongst all the rest of the apostles he alone followed Him to the cross; but chiefly for this cause, that when He was upon the cross He committed His mother unto him, in whom only, as you yourselves do confess, the lively Church of Christ remained after Christ's death. For all the apostles were not a little afraid and dismayed with that terrible doleful sight of Christ's death upon the cross, according as Christ had told him before. And if John were not ordained the supreme head of the Church of Christ, then much less was Peter.

Then said Master Falsidicus: Will ye see how

The Tragedy

Christ ordained only Peter to be the chief pastor of all?
Luke v. Read the Gospel of Luke and there shall ye find spoken only to Peter, Thou shalt be a fisher of men.

Thereunto answered the Ambassador: And will you see how Christ ordained not Peter to be the chief pastor of all? Read the Gospel of Matthew, and Mark, and there shall ye find the same spoken also of Christ to Andrew, and the two sons of Zebedee. Wherefore it followeth that Peter only was not assigned of Christ to be the fisher of men; yea, and consequently not alone of His own sheep. Christ never said to Peter only, Feed thou my sheep; be thou only a fisher of men; to thee only will I give the keys of the kingdom of Heaven. No; He never said so much as this, Be thou only a shepherd and a fisher above the rest of the apostles; take thou more authority than they have. But He said in simple and plain words, I will give unto thee the keys of the kingdom of Heaven, and so He kept promise. Marry! He gave the same keys also to the rest of the
The keys were not given only to Peter. apostles. And that this is true it is evident. For Christ gave the keys to Peter and to the rest of the apostles after His resurrection from death, standing in the midst of them, when He had saluted them and showed His hands and His side, that they should both see and know Him that talked with them and delivered them the keys, to be indeed very Christ the Son of God. He said

The Tragedy

unto them, as John writeth, Even as my Father sent me, so send I you. As though He had said, My Father hath sent me into this world that I should preach the Gospel, as Esay the prophet said long ago. Therefore do I send you even of the same fashion, throughout the world to preach these glad tidings, that I am nailed upon the cross and dead for the sins of the whole world; that I am the only and everlasting Redemption and Reconciler, who have purchased the favour of the Eternal Father to all mankind by the price and ransom of my blood, and that all the sins of all the men in the world be pardoned and blotted out for my sake. The selfsame sentence Mark expressed, albeit it were in other words, when he showeth how Christ, after His resurrection from death, said to His apostles going throughout the universal world, Preach the Gospel to all creatures. And Matthew, Go forth, teach all people. Luke writeth that Christ said, It is written, and therefore it must be, that Christ shall suffer and rise again from death the third day, in whose name repentance and remission of sins must be preached to all people, beginning at Jerusalem. It is plain that the evangelists agree hitherto. John furthermore doth add that Christ said unto them, Take ye the Holy Ghost; which thing Luke declareth after another sort, saying that Christ opened their minds that they might understand the Scriptures,

Mark xvi.

Matt. xxvi.
Luke xxiiii.

The Tragedy

which is the very true office of the Holy Ghost. Wherefore He gave them the Holy Ghost, breathing upon them; that is (as Luke doth declare), He opened their minds and knowledge that they might understand the Holy Scriptures; and that was so done that they might know and perceive that the Gospel which they should preach was no vain or new thing, but true and of antiquity, spoken of before by the unfeigned sayings of the prophets. Which thing they believing undoubtedly, through an earnest stirring and motion of the Holy Ghost, should preach the Gospel throughout the whole world. Now afterward when He gave them the keys, John writeth that He said, Whose sins soever ye forgive, they be forgiven them; and whose sins soever ye retain, they be retained. That is to say, I deliver you the keys of the kingdom of Heaven, and give you authority and power to open and shut the same. By the kingdom of Heaven He understandeth the kingdom of grace and the kingdom of glory. The sinful man was driven out of the kingdom of the heavenly favour, neither can he find any means or ways to enter into the same again but by faith. According to the doctrine of Paul, he cannot believe of the common sort unless he hear the word of the Gospel, which cannot be without preaching. So that there was authority given unto the apostles, and keys delivered unto them,

Romans i.

Romans iiii.

Romans x.

The Tragedy

that they should open the kingdom of Heaven to the wicked, when Christ gave them authority to preach the Gospel, that is to say, to teach that men be saved by Christ. Because that when they were sinners, and without the kingdom of the grace of Christ, neither had any way opened whereby they might enter, the apostles, in preaching the Gospel, opened the gate of the favour and grace of God unto them, which guided them in the ready and plain way, whereby they might obtain to themselves the favour of God by believing that Christ died for them, by whose means and help they are saved. The apostles did move and stir men to give credit to this truth. And such of them as believed, entered into the kingdom of Christ by faith, and the apostles opened the gate unto them by preaching the word of the Gospel, and did open the way for their entry. But if the hearers of this preaching believed not, the apostles did shut the gates of God's favour, when they taught in their preaching that unless they believed the Gospel there was no hope of salvation, neither any other way or means whereby they might enter the kingdom of the favour of God, notwithstanding they had done as many good works as be in the whole world. And so is this opening and shutting, as a man may call it, a loosing and a binding, as Christ declared, when He said to Peter, To thee will I give the keys of the kingdom of Heaven. Whatsoever thou

The Tragedy

^{Matt. xvi.} shalt bind in earth, shall be bound in heaven; and whatsoever thou loosest in earth, shall be also loosed in heaven. Now these keys and power to open and shut, to loose and bind, were given to the apostles when Christ said unto them, Whose sins ye forgive, they shall be forgiven; and whose sins ye retain, they shall be retained. Not that the apostles themselves should have power and authority to pardon and forgive sin, for that belongeth to God alone. And that should be a wonderful idolatry and blasphemy to attribute and assign that thing to man which belongeth to God only; who is only He that forgiveth sins for Christ's sake, even as it is only He which poureth faith into us; and men be His servants and ministers in that they preach the Gospel and move men to believe. But the believing itself and the faith itself, and the remission of sin which is by it ^{Ephes. ii.} procured, is the gift of God. Then the apostles had no power to remit and retain sins at their own will and pleasure, neither to loose and bind, neither yet to bring man in or out of the kingdom of God, when they lusted so to do; but they had power to preach the Gospel, and to show that this preaching must be believed, and that this Gospel must be embraced with a sound faith, if they intend to have forgiveness of sins at God's hands, and so to be loosed, and to enter into the kingdom of grace. For they only have their sins forgiven

The Tragedy

them which believe the Gospel; they only be loosed and enter into the kingdom of God. They had also authority to declare that their sins were retained, which believed not the Gospel, and that they only be bound and shut out of the kingdom of God. It is evident and plain by Saint Luke Luke xxiiii. that this is the will and mind of Christ, who declareth the selfsame sentence with more plain words, saying, Christ said to His apostles that Christ must die, as it was written, and rise again the third day from death, and that repentance and remission of sin must be preached to all nations in His name. So that by this it is easy to be perceived that Christ gave His apostles keys and power, not properly to forgive sin, but to preach remission of sins to all them that believe through Christ. The selfsame thing may also be confirmed by the authority of Saint Mark, who, expounding the same sentence (although it be in other words) saith: that Christ said to His apostles, Go throughout the whole world, and preach the Gospel to all creatures; whoso believeth and is baptized shall be saved, and he that believeth not shall be damned. Whereby it may be well perceived that the authority and power which Christ gave unto His apostles was not to save and condemn, but only to preach the Gospel, and to show the way of salvation, in that they moved men to enter into that way, and they declared

The Tragedy

him to be within the compass of condemnation which gave no credit to the Gospel, and went about to dissuade men from this unbelief. These be the keys; this is the power which Christ gave to the apostles, and not only to His apostles, but also unto all their successors. Which thing doth evidently appear by the words of Christ, when He saith to His apostles, That which I say to you, I say to all. Neither seemeth it anything likely that He spake that thing which He taught to them only, but to all. Truly this is certain, as Saint Jerome wrote upon this saying (To thee will I give the keys of the heavenly kingdom), that the bishops and priests have thought hitherto, by the reason of their pride and pharisaical arrogancy, that they had power to condemn the guiltless, and to deliver the guilty. But truly they be deceived all over the field; because that the question is not before God of the judgment of the priest, but of the life of the sinner. Whereby He plainly declareth that the choice of binding and loosing is not left in the liberty of the priest, but in the sinner, who is commanded to believe. The minister of God's word doth not absolve, but he publisheth and declareth man to be absolved; and likewise he declareth man to be bound and condemned unless he believe. Even as the sceptre royal signifies a king's power and the sword the empire, so likewise doth the keys betoken the spiritual governance of the kingdom of

Mark xiii.

The Tragedy

God. For whosoever he be that preach the Gospel, be it whosoever ye will, in that he preacheth, he doeth all that lieth in him to open the kingdom of Heaven to the hearers, whether it be openly or privately, that he preach to one or to many. Moreover, he delivereth all the believers, he forgiveth all their sins, he saveth them, and bringeth them into the kingdom of God, when he teacheth that they be free by faith; and because they believe that their sins be forgiven them, they be saved and in the kingdom of Christ. Again, on the other side, he bindeth all them that believe not; he retaineth their sins; he condemneth them and shutteth them out of the kingdom of Heaven, when he teacheth them that they are bound, that they remain in their sin, that they be damned and shut out of the kingdom of grace by reason of their unbelief. But this thing is worthy to be noted, that there are two kingdoms of Christ on earth, whereof the one is spiritual and cannot be seen, wherein dwell only the godly and righteous men; and another that is much greater, wherein abide not only the good, but also all other that be baptized, which will seem to be Christians. Neither were the keys of both these kingdoms delivered only to Peter, but also to all the rest of the apostles, and by them to the successors of the apostles, that the ministers of the word of God might not only shut and open the first kingdom (as it is before

The Tragedy

declared), but also the second. For they may suspend and excommunicate sinners openly, when they amend not, after such order as Christ hath appointed, and so shut them out of the second kingdom, and banish them the company of other Christians. They may also loose, when they show forth tokens of penance; that is to say, they may declare in the Christian congregation that they be free, even as before they declared them to be bound; and by that means open unto them

Matt. xvi. and xviii.

the second kingdom, and grant unto them the liberty to dwell and abide in the company of other Christians, and with them to receive the Holy

John xx. c.

Sacraments. Then were these the keys and this the authority that Christ spake of when He said to His apostles, Whatsoever ye shall bind in earth, shall be bound in heaven; and whatsoever ye shall loose in earth, it shall be loosed also in heaven. The ministers also of the Church of Christ may and ought to enjoin penance to such as be excommunicated at such time as they convert and repent, that they may openly show tokens of a penitent heart, not that they may think thereby to satisfy and make a sufficient recompense for their offences in the sight of God, for the which Christ had suffered long ago, that neither they themselves, neither others following their example, should any more commit the like offences, neither should withstand the correction of the Church and of the

The Tragedy

ministers. But as touching the signs that be unknown and secret, the ministers ought not scrupulously to inquire for the knowledge of them. Nevertheless, the man that is troubled with this kind of sins, and coming to a sober and learned minister in Christian knowledge, telling him of the trouble of his conscience, and requiring of him what were best for him to do, whereby to be restored again to God's mercy; then shall this physician preach to the soul so repentant the Gospel, and move him to believe that Christ is He who hath satisfied for his sins, and also for the sins of the whole world. Which thing when the sinner believeth, immediately the minister of God's word openeth unto him the kingdom of Heaven and beareth witness that his sins be now forgiven him, and also the sinner so repentant may make a rehearsal and a confession of his faith before the said learned minister, and may demand of him whether that be a true and lively faith, which shall suffice to salvation. Then shall this minister open unto him the whole doctrine of Christ's faith, and so induce him to the true faith, and show him whereby he may attain to the right faith, and remain therein increasing continually. Then shall the minister open unto him remedies meet for him whereby he may preserve himself safe and unspotted from such grievous offences as he perceiveth him most inclined unto. And whoso hath

Esay liii. c.
Romans iii. c.
1 John ii. c.

The Tragedy

a true faith, goeth straightways to Christ with the Samaritan to render present thanks in His presence. But whoso hath not that faith, he shall always be a wicked man and an infidel, though he confess himself every day a thousand times. This is the power which Christ gave not only to Peter, but to all the apostles of His Church, that is to say, to preach the Gospel, to declare the remission of sins to all them that believe, and to hold in sin such as believe not; to minister the sacraments according to the Word of God and Christ's institution, and to punish them that offend openly, and will not repent, when they be entreated after such a sort as Christ hath appointed. That is, first, that they be excommunicate, and then, if they amend, to be received again into the Christian congregation. This power being given by Christ unto His Church is not extended, but to them only which be in this life, whilst they live here. And therefore said Christ, Whatsoever ye shall bind or whatsoever ye shall loose (not indifferently in all places, but in earth) shall be bound and loosed. Wherefore it is true that the Church Militant hath no power upon them that be passed out of this life and rest in the Lord. Neither gave He any authority to the Church Militant to give pardons *ab poena et culpa*, neither to ordain new kinds of worshippings, neither to devise new doctrines, or to make new articles of the faith, or to devise new command-

margin notes: Matt. xx. / Matt. xxiiii. c. / Mark. xvi. b. / Matt. xviii. b. / Matt. xvi. c. and xviii. b. / John x. c.

The Tragedy

ments, and that upon such a condition that men's consciences must be forced and tied to believe the same wicked decrees of men with a tyrannical pain even to the death, to the sword, to the flame, and fire appointed for the transgressors of the same ordinances. Christ said to His apostles, Ye shall be my witnesses, not only in Jerusalem but also in Jewry and Samaria, even to the uttermost parts of the world. And it is plain that witnesses must testify the truth, and neither add nor take away from the same any word; namely, when as the Church of Christ is His spouse, and she must be obedient unto Him, as to her husband, and speak those words only which she heareth of Him. For Christ opened to His apostles and to the first beginning of His Church all things that seemed profitable and necessary to the obtaining of salvation; wherefore He said to His disciples, I have disclosed all things unto you that I have received of my Father. The Holy Ghost opened their minds that they might understand the Scriptures, and informed and taught them all such things as Christ had said unto them. So that it cannot be without a very heinous offence that anything should be added to the doctrine of Christ and the apostles, and of the first most pure and sincere Church. Wherefore either Christ is a liar when He saith that He taught all; or else were the apostles wicked, in that they did not put the rest of the

Margin notes: Acts i., ii. Luke xxiv. John xvi. Ephes. v. John xv. Luke xxiv. John xiv.

The Tragedy

articles of our faith into the Creed which the Bishops of Rome boast they could find out afterward, and that such articles (as they say) as be very necessary, besides a great number of precepts which they have invented. The evangelists also should have been wicked creatures to keep hid things so necessary to our salvation. But neither were the apostles wicked, neither Christ a liar; for both Christ taught all things necessary, and they delivered the same to men accordingly. And Christ commanded them precisely that they should teach the people to observe and keep all those things, not which they dreamed themselves, but which He commanded them. Yea, and Paul the Apostle determined all creatures, not human only, but celestial also and angelical, to be accursed which preach any other Gospel than the Gospel of Christ. We be all born anew by the Word of God, by which thing only, as by a perfect and strong nourishment, we live and continue.

Now then, when Master Falsidicus thought the keys to be taken out of the Pope's hands by unanswerable reasons, by and by he clapped his hands upon his weapon, saying, Read Saint Luke, and ye shall see how Christ willed the disciples to provide for themselves two swords; who making answer that they had twain in a readiness, Christ said that they were enough. Therefore hath the Pope two swords, and the highest power

Matt. xxviii.

Mark. xvi.

Gala. i.

Luke xxii. c.

The Tragedy

upon both sides, the one spiritual, the other temporal.

MASSUCCIUS. O what a fine dialectical wit was that! Truly this consequence and reason could not be answered to. Verily I marvel much why they have not caused this long time Saint Peter to be painted with keys hanging upon his girdle, and holding two swords in his hands, the one in the right, and the other in the left, to declare his chief prerogative, and so to make men afraid with that fearful sight. But tell me, I pray you, what answered the Ambassador to this?

LEPIDUS. He answered that Christ promised and gave to Peter and the apostles keys, and not swords; and that when Peter used a sword for the defence of his master, Christ Himself stayed his unadvised rashness. Because the kingdom of Christ is not of this world, neither is it worldly and earthly, but heavenly and spiritual. Neither was He sent of His Father to reign in this world of a carnal fashion, as in a kingdom; but He was sent to minister and serve, and to give His life for our salvation. And forasmuch as He sent His apostles, even of a like fashion as He Himself was sent of His Father, He sent them not as though they should reign in the world, but to be like innocent lambs amongst wolves. And to mind to establish one supreme head, in the Church of Christ, is nothing else but a crowning again of Christ with a crown of

John xviii. c.

Matt. xx. and xxviii.

Mark x. e.

Luke xxii. b.

Matt. x. b.

The Tragedy

thorns, and when He is apparelled with a purple and a kingly vesture, to deliver Him to men to be made a laughing-stock, as He was scorned in times past of the Jews, when He hung upon the cross. Therefore Christ foreseeing that His apostles would be offended with His death, and would slip from that trust they had in Him (as He prophesied to them before), He demanded of them whether they wanted any manner of thing when He sent them forth naked and destitute of all men's help. And when they answered that they wanted nothing, He said, Now then provide you for swords, as though He had said, Hitherto have I been your merciful master and governor. I have defended you. I have provided all necessaries for you as for my beloved children; ye lacked nothing; I took the tuition of you. But because within this short space, when ye shall see me caught by the hands of the wicked, and bound, and in conclusion die, ye will be offended with that miserable sight, and will faint from that sure trust that ye have had in me hitherto, it is needful that from henceforth ye provide for yourselves; and therefore I give you warning to prepare ye swords for your defence, for the persecution that cometh upon you shall be great. And when they showed two swords and said, Master, lo, here be two swords! Christ answered them rebukingly with a privy check, saying, They be enough. This was a wonderful

The Tragedy

declaration and figure of the dulness of the apostles and of the clemency of Christ. Even as though tender infants showed their father two spears made of reeds, and then asked of him whether those spears of reed were sufficient to overcome an exceeding strong army; unto whom the father should answer with a smiling countenance, saying, Yea, they be sufficient. As though he had said, O, ye tenderlings! think you that spears of reed can prevail without my help? Now is it here evident, first and foremost, that Christ gave not swords to His apostles; whereof it followeth that He gave them not the supreme power and authority, both spiritual and temporal, which is shadowed (as you hold opinion) by these two swords. And, moreover, Peter only made not the answer, Lo, here be two swords, but the disciples, as Luke plainly doth witness. Neither is it read anywhere that Peter alone hath two swords. And although it were so that the highest supremacy were shadowed by these two swords, yet may ye not by any means infer or go about to prove that the same authority belonged only to Peter, but to all the apostles jointly, and the whole Church together. And yet cannot I perceive how these reasons hang together: Christ said checkingly that two swords were enough; ergo, Peter had the supreme authority, both spiritual and temporal, given unto him.

Then would Master Falsidicus without doubt

Gen. ix. a.
Ex. ix. a.
Matt. xxvi.
John xviii.
Apoc. xiii.

The Tragedy

have made some pretty answer, as his fashion is, if the Pope had not commanded him to hold his peace; fearing lest this hateful disputation of both swords should offend the Emperor. Whereof he said to Falsidicus that it was sufficient for this present to retain the one sword, that is to say, the chief dominion in spiritual matters, and to permit the other, of temporal matters, to Cæsar's Majesty.

MASSUCCIUS. A wonderful liberality!

LEPIDUS. But ye must know that he granted this but for a time, yea, and against his will. For his left arm is weak and small, because he is not accustomed to use it. But let him alone and suffer his strength with a little exercise to come to him, and ye shall see him, halt and lame as he is, shed more blood alone than all the emperors of the world, though ye put them together.

Then Master Falsidicus, finding other matters to talk upon, said : You know right well, Master Ambassador, that Christ keepeth promise. And if He give a name to any man, at any time, that name is not a void name. It is not the bare sound of a voice, but the truth of the thing itself is also agreeable to the name. And because Christ said to Simon, From henceforth thou shalt be called Cephas, which by interpretation signifieth a head; ye must of necessity grant that Christ gave in deed that which He promised with special and plain words. Simon was called Cephas, that is to say, a head;

Matt. xxvi. c.

John i. d.

The Tragedy

then it followeth that he was a head by the name that Christ gave him; ergo, he was a head indeed, that the truth might be agreeable to his name.

To this the Ambassador answered:

Truly ye be worthy to be burned; for if ye burn them which deprave the writings of the apostles, what ought ye to do to them which pervert falsely the words of Christ Himself? Christ said to Peter, Thou shalt be called Cephas; and Cephas is a word of the language of the Syrians; which is as much to say as Petra, that is, a stone. But you, depraving the Holy Scriptures, say that Christ said, Thou shalt be called a head; and this do you to the end that you would draw all sentences (as though it were hauling them by the neck), writhing[1] them to your perverse purpose, and in the meantime corrupting the truth and the majesty of Holy Scriptures.

MASSUCCIUS. I marvel that he was ever afterwards called Peter, and not rather head, if it be so that this name Cephas signify a head, and not Petra, which is a stone, as Master Falsidicus did contend. But tell me, I pray you, was not he ashamed to speak any more?

LEPIDUS. Nay; then he seemed but as it were to begin to prove the primacy of Peter.

MASSUCCIUS. And what thing brought he therefore?

---

[1] *Writhing*, wresting or twisting.

The Tragedy

LEPIDUS. First and foremost, thus he said, Even as it is evident by the Scriptures of the Old Testament that the first begotten was the lord over all his brethren, even so because it is evident that Peter was the first begotten of Christ, he must be lord over all the rest, and supreme head of the whole Church of Christ, which thing may be proved by that, that Peter, as the chief and most worthy person, speaketh always first for them all ; and amongst the rest he was always accounted and named the first. Yea, be it that it could not be proved by any word of God that Peter was declared supreme head by Christ, yet ought we to believe it, forasmuch as we must assuredly persuade ourselves that Christ ordained His Church well, and therefore that it was done by a certain reason and order ; for where as a certain order is not observed, there must all things of force be full of confusion ; and certain order can there none be, whereas there be not degrees of men higher and lower. But where as there is a higher degree of men, there must ye ascend and come to me, as to a supreme head, that the nature of order may be preserved, which because it cannot proceed so far but that it must have an end, unless there should be some supreme head established it should come altogether to nothing. Now likely it is not that Christ appointed any other head than Peter ; ergo, Peter was the supreme head. The selfsame

The Tragedy

thing may be proved of the order of natural things, where all things be referred to one, as to a chief beginning and original cause. For not only in any civil governance of man (if the commonwealth be well ordered) there is supreme head, but amongst brute beasts also we see this dignity of order observed. Bees have their king,[1] who govern the baser sort of the common people, and oversee them to do their duties. The cranes have one chief guide whom all the rest doth follow. The sheep also have their shepherd, whose voice they know, and whom they follow, and at whose commandment they be. So that look, how much the Church of Christ is more excellent and more perfect than other things that belong to man, and is also better governed. So much is it the more likely, that there must be one supreme head in it at whose commandment all men must hang, as though he were a god. John x.

To these reasons the Ambassador made answer:

If the first begotten amongst the apostles ought to be lord of all the rest (as Falsidicus said even now), forasmuch as Andrew was called before Peter to the office of the apostleship, Peter should not take the lordship away from him which of right should have a better title to it. But truth it is that Christ is the first begotten amongst His

---

[1] *King*, probably used here irrespective of sex, as we still use the titles monarch, sovereign, ruler.

The Tragedy

brethren, and He is only the lord of all. And all the worthiness of the first begetting, which was shadowed in the first begotten of the Old Testament, is fulfilled in Christ Himself. Now because that the kingdom of Christ is altogether spiritual, he may be accounted greater, higher, and more excellent, not that is first born to Christ in this world, nor he that is richer or more noble after the flesh, nor he that is better learned; but he that excelleth more in godliness, but he that hath received more light and strength of the Holy Ghost. And although Peter used oftentimes to chop in and speak first, by reason of his boldness, his zeal, his earnestness, and age; yet followeth it not of that, that he had dominion and authority over the rest of the apostles, neither that he was their Pope. Neither is he which speaketh first in any congregation to be thought the head of all the rest; for then indeed should Peter have been Pope, not only before Christ gave him the keys, but also before He promised them, because that oftentimes long before that time he spake before his fellows. And Philip also, and Andrew, and Thomas, and the rest should by this reason have been Popes, all the which spake first at sundry times. And although Christ when He numbered the apostles named Peter first, yet is it not necessary that therefore he should be Pope over the rest. Even as our Bishop of Constantinople hath spoken

<small>John vi., xi., and xiiii.</small>

The Tragedy

first in sundry councils that hath been, and hath also been taken for the first bishop, because he spake first, and sat first in the congregation. And yet for all that, was he never judged bishop over all other bishops, neither yet their head (which ye challenged to you by tyranny). I grant truly that Christ did set in order and governed His Church wonderfully well, and that it hath gone forward in a wonderful order; so that I cannot deny that there must be some supreme head in that Church. But that head is Christ Himself (as Paul testifieth), who by His Spirit is present with His Church evermore, and governeth it after a more wonderful fashion than man's understanding can comprehend. Neither is it needful to dream of any other universal head in earth, for Christ Himself, without any other Popes, governeth His Church by His ministers most wonderfully. But let us grant that Christ declared Peter to be the head of the apostles and of the first Church, at the which time, because they were very few, he might right well govern them all. But now when the Church of Christ is spread abroad throughout the whole world, it is not possible for him to know them all or to visit them all, to understand their tongues, to hear their matters, to provide for them all, and govern them all well. One crane may well be the guide of other twenty-five cranes, or else peradventure fifty; but me-

The Tragedy

thinketh that it is a thing impossible that all the cranes in the world should follow this one crane as their only guide; yea, and be it that they all followed this one, yet doth not that prove that this one, being guide, is the head of all the rest. Of the like sort, say I of the bees, amongst whom it may well be and is, that one bee be king and governor of all the others that be in the same hive, as a bishop may be the governor of all the souls that be within his diocese. But yet, as it cannot be that one bee should govern all the bees of the world, so neither can it be that one Bishop of Rome can have the cure of all the souls in the world.

MASSUCCIUS. Will you have me say to you what I think? This bishop of ours seemeth to me a very ass, and without all judgment and perseverance, and this is my reason that moveth me so to say. I have seen many times and have proved by experience the thing that I shall tell: When one shepherd hath the charge of a thousand sheep, it is as much as he is able to do to feed so many and order them well; but the same shepherd cannot keep six or eight thousand, and yet much less an hundred beasts and a thousand sheep together, and yet much less a thousand sheep and beasts, an hundred oxen, an hundred kine, an hundred asses, and an hundred swine. But this bishop of ours will be the universal bishop and shepherd of all Christian men, amongst whom be found not only

The Tragedy

beasts innumerable, but asses also, and kine, boars, and swine, and an infinite number of foxes and wolves. Ye know that I am the master of his horse, and am fain some time to spend a whole month to tame one fierce beast, or before I can bring a mule to her true pace. And he will take upon him to tame all the whole world; and he thinketh to bring it to pass that all men shall walk right the same way that leadeth to God. But I pray you, tell on the disputation, for in hearing you recite godly their reasons (in the name of God) I am more and more strengthened in the truth.

LEPIDUS. He brought, moreover, an argument of the chief priest of the Jews, saying: It is plain that the Old Testament is a figure of the New. Now then, as they, by the will of God, had one chief priest above all other, so the Christian men nowadays must have one Pope. And he must be honoured and set forth with such beauty and glory that the kings of the world (as the prophets have spoken before) shall come to worship this marvellous godhead in earth. And furthermore, all Christian men shall come to Rome as to a spiritual Jerusalem, which was shadowed by that earthly Jerusalem, to obtain salvation and receive heaven at the Pope's hands. And then he said thus: Now methinketh that I have confirmed and established sufficiently the Popeship with these reasons and

The Tragedy

authorities that I have alleged. Wherefore now will I make an end and give place to other. And to conclude of this, I am sure that the Ambassador cannot find one word in the Holy Scripture that may make by any means against this primacy once planted and established.

Then the Ambassador made answer on this wise :

The Jews were but few in comparison with the Christian men, who if they were this day compared with them, they should appear innumerable. And again, they were all knit and joined together in one narrow place ; but the Christian men this day be dispersed throughout the whole world. Wherefore that thing which according to the will of God was meet for them then (that is to say, that they should have one chief priest in earth) cannot agree now with us of these days. Moreover, the high priesthood of the Jews shadowed not the high priesthood of the Bishops of Rome, but the high priesthood of Christ. Wherefore that high priesthood of the Jews after a certain time hath an end. And furthermore, the earthly Jerusalem figured not Rome, but the spiritual Church of Christ, whereunto all the chosen resort, to obtain favour and health of Christ, our chief and everlasting priest, to whom all the princes of the earth ought to come flat down and worship, that they may acknowledge and confess Him to be the Son of God. But your Rome is so far unlike to the spiritual Jerusalem

The Tragedy

that it may worthily be called filthy, and carnal Babylon, as Peter termed it. _{1 Peter v.}

MASSUCCIUS. Rome seemeth to me the very lively and express image of that great whore, of whom it is written in the Apocalypse, who hath made drunk, corrupted, and infected all the whole _{Apoc. xvii.} world with her golden cup of hypocrisy, replenished to the very brim with abomination and uncleanness. She deceiveth and blindeth the eyes of all men, with a pleasant outward deceitful show of feigned holiness, of ceremonies, of beauty, of riches, and of abundance of things that fade and decay. But tell on the end of the disputation.

LEPIDUS. When Master Falsidicus had spent all his matter, and said what he could, the Ambassador began to declare how the Holy Scripture was directly against this primacy. And first he made _{Hebrews v. 1.} it plain very well that Christ was the chief priest, not after the order of Aaron, but after the order of Melchisedech; and that He was not of the tribe of Levi or of the stock of Aaron, but of the tribe of Judah and the stock of David; and moreover, that He was not chosen as other men be, as other chief priests be chosen of other priests, who doth not always choose the best; but He was chosen of His Eternal and Heavenly Father when He said, Thou art my Son, this day have I begotten _{Psalm ii.} Thee. And the other chief priests were anointed _{Hebrews v.} with a material oil, but Christ was anointed with

The Tragedy

the Holy Ghost. And they had on such garments as Moses appointed them by God's commandment, but the apparel of Christ was the whole company of all virtues. They offered incense and brute beasts, but Christ offered Himself upon the cross with a spiritual and heavenly excellent sweet savour. They entered the Holy of Holies, but Christ entered into Heaven, and sitteth now at the right hand of the Eternal Father, making intercession for us, obtaining whatsoever He desireth. Whereas beforetime He did put upon Him our infirmities, that by the means thereof He might be earnestly sorrowful for our miseries. So that Christ was chief priest after the order of Melchisedech, which was much more excellent than was the order of Aaron. Neither was He only the Son of God, unto whom the Spirit is given without measure, and all power and dominion in heaven and earth, in whom all treasures of wisdom and knowledge of God be hid, who is full of grace and truth, but in whom also dwelleth a full plentifulness of heavenly things. And that Christ hath now taken away Aaron's priesthood as a thing imperfect, and was but a shadow¹ of this, which is more perfect. So that they now may be accounted true priests, which be regenerated by Christ, and have the Spirit of God; and them to be the greater and better priests, who have received a greater measure and abundance

Margin references: Exodus xxviii. Esay lxi. Hebrews ix. and vii. Esay liii. Romans iii. Gala. iii. 1 Tim. ii. John xvii. 1 John ii. Hebrews v. John iv. 1. Matt. xxviii. John xiii. Coloss. ii. John i. Coloss. i.

---
¹ *Shadow*, prefiguration or type.

The Tragedy

of that heavenly Spirit; and all the other to be profane and wicked, notwithstanding that they be a thousand times anointed, ordered, and chosen into the number of priests by the Pope and his members. Wherefore he saith, Either ye have the Spirit or not. If ye have not the Spirit of God, then be ye no priests, neither after the order of Melchisedech, neither after the order of Aaron, because ye be not of his family. Therefore can ye not be priests but after the order of Belial, after whose order ye may well be the chief priests of all. But if ye have the Spirit of God, then be ye right precious indeed, and him shall ye think to be the highest priest of all who is replenished with more abundance of the Spirit of God. And because that Christ only received the Spirit without measure, He only must be taken for the true, only, and chief high priest. And forasmuch as Christ only is full of light, grace, truth, power, and all heavenly virtue, it were an extreme wickedness, idolatry, and abomination to study to rob Christ of these heavenly gifts, and appoint them to a mortal man; and so much the more and greater should the abomination be, the more we be assured that Christ is the chief everlasting priest, as David prophesied, Psalm xix. and as it is written to the Hebrews. Wherefore Hebrews vii. as the chief priest of the Jews died, and another was appointed in his place, by the means whereof they were many; so this Christ, our eternal priest, being

The Tragedy

once raised from death, dieth no more, but is ascended into Heaven, where now He liveth and reigneth chief priest for ever, and is able perfectly to save all those that come forth into the sight of God, trusting upon His mediation. It is the office of the chief priest to put himself between God and the people, to offer for the sins of men, to pray for them, and to purchase the favour of God unto them. But now since Christ hath offered Himself upon the cross for our sins, and hath pacified the wrath of God for ever, and hath preserved His chosen once for all, that we shall not more have any need of high priests, which should offer again for our offences. If that, after all this, we attempt to do sacrifice again for this end, it cannot be done without an exceeding great injury of God, and open contempt of the sacrifice of Christ. We have no need at this present to have any other men to put themselves between us and God as chief priests, because that we obtain all favour by Christ only and alone, as by our only chief priest, chief head, and mediator, by whose means, and for whose sake, our prayer, works, and sacrifices be not only accepted, but ourselves also. Wherefore Christ only and alone is sufficient for us, neither have we need of any other chief priests, because it is a dignity that no man living can use without a great offence of God. Who knoweth not that Christ only is called of the Holy Ghost the head of His

Hebrews x.

1 Tim. ii.

The Tragedy

Church, not only of the Church Militant, but of the Church Triumphant? Wherein He shall reign for ever until the latter day of judgment. Even as it is necessary that He should reign until He hath put His enemies a footstool to His feet. Christ will have this high dignity of the supreme head in His Church reserved full and whole to Himself; as He is the true foundation of His Church, unto whom only this dignity worthily agreeth, because He is the only One which as One Supreme Head hath the fulness of the treasures, and of the knowledge and wisdom of God, and of His favour and all virtue. This is He alone, who, having the Spirit without measure, ruleth and governeth His Church as a universal head, giving to other men, as to His inferior members, sundry gifts and benefits after a certain proportion and measure. Wherefore even as in the spiritual Church of Christ they only be true priests who have the gift of the Holy Ghost poured upon them, and they be the greater priests which have the same in a more plentiful measure; and Christ is the only chief priest who hath the Spirit without measure: of a like sort they only be true and lively members of the body of the same Church, which have the Spirit of God; and they be more noble and more worthy, who have the same Spirit more abundantly. And Christ only is their head who chiefly and most abundantly hath the Spirit of the Eternal Father. Wherefore,

1 Peter ii.
Ephes. iiii.
Luke ii.
1 Cor. xv.
Ephes. iiii.

The Tragedy

in that the Bishop of Rome intendeth to attain to the dignity of the chief priest and supreme head of Christ's Church, his study is nothing else but to make himself equal with Christ in spirit, knowledge, virtue, power, and in all other gifts and graces. Now whether this be a blasphemous mind or not, judge you. For that man which hath not the Spirit of God is not worthy to be called a member of Christ, or a priest, or else a Christian man. No, he is not worthy the name of a man for his grievous offences. Yea, he ought to be banished from all Christian men's company, and be excommunicated from the Church of Christ. It cannot be without a marvellous heinous offence, and a devilish pride, one to be so bold to desire to have the title of the supreme head of the Church of Christ. Whereas Paul describeth the true image of the Church of Christ. He saith, Christ is ascended on high, and hath given gifts to men ; some to be apostles, some to be prophets, some to be evangelists, and some to be doctors. And it is not to be doubted, but He would also have ordained some other supreme head in earth, if He had judged it a thing necessary. And the Holy Ghost in this place (which should have made so much for this purpose) would not only have expressed the thing by the mouth of Paul, but would also have named this chief dignity. When Paul mindeth to persuade the Ephesians to remain together in one

Ephes. iiii.
Psalm i.
1 Cor. xix.

The Tragedy

spirit, knit with the bond of peace, the arguments that he useth be these, saying, that (if they be true Christian men) they be the very members of one body, and they all have one spirit, even as they all be called to one end, and have one Lord Jesus Christ, one faith, one baptism, one only God and one Father. No doubt he would have also said in this place, And they have one bishop in earth who keepeth the Church of Christ in order and concord, if he had ever minded to appoint such a bishop. *Ephes. iiii.*

MASSUCCIUS. If Paul had ever spoken such words he had lied gallantly. For the Bishops of Rome will endeavour of themselves to the uttermost of their power to move contention and to set Christian princes together by the ears for their own enriching.

LEPIDUS. That thing may chance to be true. But I pray you let me tell on my tale. Then the Ambassador said furthermore, It is not unknown unto you that when the congregation of the Corinthians announced themselves sometimes in the name of Peter, sometimes in the name of Paul, and sometimes of Apollo, and Paul chid them bitterly for so doing, he said not, I will not have you think hereafter that I am the head of the Church, neither yet Apollo, but Peter only. But he rather concluded all manner of men, and said thus: What? were you baptized in the name of Paul? Was Paul ever crucified for you? As though he had *Cor. i. and iii. a.* *1 Cor. i. b.*

The Tragedy

said, Truly ye be neither baptized in the name of Paul, neither in the name of Peter, neither of Apollo, neither was there any of them crucified for you; but ye be baptized in Christ's name only. Only He suffered for you death upon the cross. Only He hath redeemed you and saved you from sin. Only He is your head, from which all heavenly gifts descend. Only He is your light, your wisdom, your life, your salvation, and therefore must ye acknowledge Him only and alone to be your supreme head, in whose name only ye must rejoice. And then to knit up his disputation, he said not, Man must esteem and take Apollo and me for the ministers of Christ, and Peter for the lord and master; but putting Peter and himself and Apollo all together, he said, Man must take us as the ministers of Christ. And in this point he agreeth with the doctrine of Christ, who perceiving His apostles to contend among themselves for the highest place, because they heard say that James and John had obtained a prerogative of Christ by the procurement of their mother, that one of them should sit at His right hand, and the other at His left, said, Ye know right well that the princes of nations bear lordly rule, and men of power do exercise their might over them. But it shall not be so amongst you. But he that will be greater amongst you shall be your minister, and he that will be chief amongst

1 Cor. iiii.

The Tragedy

you shall be your servant. For the Son of Man came not to be served of other, but to serve other Himself, and to give His soul for a redemption for many. Whereby it is easy to perceive that the Church of Christ is altogether spiritual. And it is not possible that any man can be a true priest, neither a true Christian man in this spiritual Church of Christ, unless he have the Spirit of God, and he is to be thought greater that is more enriched with strength and abundance of the Spirit. So that forasmuch as Christ only hath the greatest plentifulness of the Spirit, He must without controversy be judged and esteemed the chief and head priest of all other. Wherefore if the Bishop of Rome desire the place of the chief bishop, he must of necessity have greatest abundance of the Spirit, even as Christ had; and then, when he is equal with Christ, he shall also be chief bishop and chief head, equal with Christ. But this is necessary also to be known, that the dominion of the Spirit is very diverse and contrary (even as Christ taught) to the dominion of the flesh; for amongst carnal men, such as have more riches, more strength, more favour amongst men, more friendship and more nobility of blood, they be lords over other; they command, they have other ministers to them, they be honoured and obeyed, and many times they oppress the weaker and use tyranny over them. But it is contrariwise in the spiritual Church

The Tragedy

of Christ ; for such as have greater light of the Spirit, they be higher and greater. And they that be such, serve all other by the help of the Spirit, as men that hath received greater gifts of God, more light of knowledge, more grace, more spirit, and a greater talent. So that he which hath received more abundance of the Spirit helpeth more, and serveth more the necessities of other, and setteth forth the glory of God more plentifully. And because Christ had most singular plenty of the Spirit, therefore came not He to be served, but

Matt. xx. d. to serve for the health of His chosen. Yea, and He served all without exception, and that also humbling

Mark x. e. Himself extremely, until that He (moved of an ex-
Luke xxii. d. ceeding great love) spent His own life upon the cross. Therefore would Christ have it known to His chosen, that if ye will have a true nobility and

Phil. ii. a. worthiness, ye must have a spirit. Christ abused not this spiritual greatness of His, which was in the highest degree of honour, thereby to challenge any honour before man, or for the obtaining of riches, or imperiously to use the service of His subjects, neither to seek for any private commodity, but to serve other and to seek for the profit of other. The power, therefore, and the greatness of the ministers of Christ is altogether spiritual, and standeth wholly in the service and governance of souls' health. But the Bishop of Rome seeketh for no other thing than to be esteemed great before

The Tragedy

the world, that he may be worshipped in earth, as it were a god, and have liberty to use tyranny over all churches, to spoil and destroy them at his pleasure. If the Church of Christ were now as in times past it was ordained to be, he should be thought greater than all the rest who is endowed with more light from above, and hath received more gifts and benefits of God's hand, and this worthiness of his would he only use in setting forth of the Gospel, whereby he might win as many souls as might be to Christ. So that be it that Christ hath given the power of the keys of the kingdom of Heaven to Peter only, and by him to you that be Bishops of Rome (which thing is not true), what other power or authority should you have thereby (I pray you) than to preach the Gospel, than to be witnesses that sins be pardoned to them that believe, and retained to them that believe not; than to administer the sacraments according to Christ's institution; than to exhort, to admonish, to correct with gentleness and love such as be prone to sin; than to excommunicate (which is the chief matter of all) such as be open, notorious sinners, when they amend not after monition given according to the doctrine of Christ, and will not obey the Church? Thus far extendeth your power and authority given by Christ, and no further, except ye will confound the bounds and the order of the power civil and the power ecclesiastical.

The Tragedy

MASSUCCIUS. This confusion should not our bishop in any way suffer, and that for two causes. The first, because he will have all his power esteemed of men to be spiritual and heavenly, although he overrun the whole world with his unbridled tyranny. The latter, because if he would say that the ecclesiastical power might be mingled and confounded with power civil, he might be afraid lest haply the Emperor should challenge them both, and so be made both Emperor and Pope. I remember that I have heard tell how Christ was desired of a fellow to make division of inheritance between him and his brother, unto whom Christ made answer, "Who made me your judge? Who gave me authority to divide the inheritance between you?" As though He had said, I came not, neither am I sent of my Heavenly Father, that I should challenge to me any political power, but spiritual only. I come to preach unto you the whole spiritual kingdom, and to bring you to that highness of mind, that ye should leave not only the world, but yourself also, for the glory of God, and not to be an arbiter or judge of your strifes.

Luke xii. b.

If therefore our bishop were Pope never so much (as he striveth to be) and Christ's vicar on earth, it is very true, that he hath no more power or authority given him by Christ than had Christ Himself. And therefore whensoever there should be any civil matters brought before him in judgment, he should make answer with Christ, Who made me your judge? Or else, Who gave me authority to divide or put together, to absolve or condemn by a civil fashion of judgment? This power must come some other ways than by Christ. But I fear me much lest our Popes shall by this their new authority be so much occupied in worldly businesses that they shall have no space to think any whit of God. And moreover, so much shall their tyranny increase that they shall willingly desire, and draw to themselves and to their judgment-seats, all manner of controversies, not to make an end of them, but to involve them and make them more doubtful, by the means whereof the suits endure the longer. And furthermore, when they be once made drunk with the blood of martyrs, they will sow deadly discord and continual contention amongst Christian princes, and will be the authors almost of all wars which shall continue for many years. For it is not possible that commonwealths should be quiet where they shall have rule. But I pray you tell me in good earnest, brought the Ambassador any other authority of Scripture against the Popeship?

LEPIDUS. He brought amongst others, as far as I remember, the authority of Saint Paul, who wrote to the Galatians that Peter was the apostle of the Jews, even as Paul was of the Gentiles. Where-

The Tragedy

Gala. ii. b. fore he was neither the apostle (said he) neither the Pope of Rome, neither any of other nations, but of the Jews only; neither was he universal Bishop of all Christendom; neither you that be the Bishops of Rome be the successors of Peter, because ye be not the apostles nor bishops of the Jews. But Paul should rather have been Pope of the Gentiles, and so much the more above Peter, because that the Gentiles, of whom Paul was the apostle, were more in number than were the Jews, and more of the Gentiles were converted to Christ than of the Jews. And Paul preached also in sundry places of the world and brought forth the fruit of the Gospel more plentifully than did Peter; wherefore he was an apostle more universal and more profitable also to the Church of Christ. And Paul, moreover, addeth this thing in the same place, that he had no less grace, being the apostle of the Gentiles, than Peter had, being the apostle of the Jews. Then was not Peter a greater apostle than Paul was. And so consequently doth it follow that he was not his head; yea, and Paul doth plainly call him, in special words, fellow, even as

1 Peter v. he did both James and John. And Peter also, writing to the pastors of other churches, commandeth them, not imperiously as though he were their superior, but exhorteth them gently, as his fellows,

Gala. ii. calling Christ and not himself the chief pastor. And furthermore, when he was rebuked of Paul,

The Tragedy

he said not that he was above all laws, and could not err because he was Pope; but gave place to Paul when he was checked of him openly. And also when he was sent by the apostles into Samaria he withstood them not. He said not, It is my office to command; I have authority to send whom I will, or else to go my ways if it please me, for I am your head. But he obeyed their commandments as a member of the Church of Christ. <small>Acts viii.</small>

And when the Ambassador would have followed his matter that he intended more at large, and have brought more places of Scripture for the better subversion of all the Popeship, then Master Falsidicus, thinking himself not well handled with the Ambassador's manifold and strong reason, interrupting his tale, past all good manners, as a madman in his fury, cried out with loud voice and said—

Ye of the East Churches be full of sects and heresies. And therefore have you of all other, most need of a supreme and visible head in earth; by whose authority and wisdom ye may be governed; by whom the contentions that arise amongst you for sundry interpretations of Scripture, may be pacified; and this thing being declared and opened by the censure and judgment of the chief bishop, by the which means ye might know the truth, and remain firm and stable in the true faith quietly. For this cause should you chiefly desire this supreme head and governor, who now labour to

The Tragedy

hinder this thing for lack of knowledge of the profit that shall ensue. And therefore cannot I stay myself, but must a little pass the bonds of patience and speak my mind freely. If the whole matter were put to me, I know what I had to do. I say no more.

To these words the Ambassador answered quietly : Master Falsidicus, Ye say if the whole matter were put to you, ye know what ye had to do. Because these words may be taken diversely, seeing you expound them not yourself, there is none of us that can well tell what ye mean by them ; some may peradventure guess, but none can have any certain assurance. So that you only know what is meant by them, even as Paul wrote, What man is he living that knoweth the inward parts, the inward thoughts, desires, and crafts of man, except it be the spirit of man that dwelleth within him? Even so because men see not the inward thoughts of men, they understand not to what end their words tend, and therefore is it no marvel if they attain not the perfect knowledge of those things that be spoken, namely when the words be doubtful and ambiguous. Therefore with what face dareth the Bishop of Rome, being a mortal man, challenge unto him authority and judgment to expound the Word of God as it shall please him, and to force men to follow his exposition, be it right or wrong ? It was the Holy Ghost and not Peter that opened

1 Cor. ii.

Luke xxiiii.

The Tragedy

the minds of the apostles, whereby they might understand the Holy Scriptures, and He taught them all His own will, as Christ promised before, and as Esay did write; they were taught of God, and the law of God was printed in their stomachs, and written in their hearts from above, as Jeremy prophesied long before, and John shadowed the same thing, saying, Ye have no need of any man's help whereby to learn, for the Anointed itself, that is to say, the Holy Ghost, shall teach you all truth. The Holy Ghost is the truest teacher of all other, and one that performeth His promise most abundantly. He is no liar, as men be that break their faith and promise; it is He only that can declare the true sense of the Holy Scripture; it is He only that can open the minds of men, that can teach, strengthen, and stablish us in all truth, and not the Bishops of Rome. And if you would say that the Pope being lightened by the Holy Ghost giveth light to us, I will answer first: The Pope is not alone lightened with the light of the Holy Ghost; for the Holy Ghost inspireth where as it pleaseth Him, and distributeth His gifts amongst men, to every one as His will is. Wherefore men's consciences must not be bounden and tied to believe and think that the Pope only hath the Holy Ghost, that the Pope only cannot err, that the Pope only is above the Word of God; that the Pope only must be the interpreter, the declarer

The Tragedy

and ruler of Holy Scripture, and that all we must obey the Pope's judgment. Because that this is once sure, that visible things can bring no inward light, nor confirm men in their faith, and quiet and pacify their consciences; but the Holy Ghost only can perform all these things plentifully. What needeth many words? He is very Antichrist which boasteth himself that he can give light to the mind either by an inward light, or by some other means than by the express Word of God, as the minister of the Word, by good example of life, and continual prayer. If all we should stand or fall by the judgment of the Pope, why is there so much labour spent in gathering together of councils? Why spend we our lives with so much pain in study for knowledge; in turning our books; if we shall lean to the only word of the Pope? Then in the name of God let us be short, let us come to the Pope and hear his word as it were an oracle, and let us worship him as a God. But Paul the Apostle teacheth far after another sort, when he commandeth two or three to speak in the Church in order one after another, and the rest diligently to weigh the judgments of them that speak. And so the judgment of ecclesiastical matters must be sought for at the Church itself, and not at the Pope of Rome. And further, Paul willeth in especial words that when one of the members of the Church speaketh, the truth be

margin: 1 Cor. xiiii.

The Tragedy

revealed to another that sitteth by: him that spake first to hold his peace (though he were Pope) and give ear unto the latter, unto whom the truth is disclosed, though he be one of the basest sort and unlearned. For many times God hideth the secrets of His wisdom from the prudent and wise of this world, and openeth the same to little ones. And in another place he maketh Peter equal with the rest, saying, All things be yours, whether it be Paul, or Apollo, or Peter, as though he should say, Let none be your superiors besides Christ and His word; for Peter and Paul be your ministers. Yea, and Peter in the first council of the apostles harkened to other declaring his own judgment in that point, and giving authority to the Church to do what they should think good, and willingly and gladly to obey the judgment which the whole congregation approveth to be perfect and sure. And although Christ said, I have prayed for thee, Peter, that thy faith should not fail, yet followeth it not that Peter could not err. For he erred after that time sundry times, and namely when he expressly denied Christ the Son of God. But when Christ perceived Peter's temerous[1] boldness, and that shortly after he would shamefully deny Him, to arm and strengthen him against the temptation which should ensue, lest the greatness of the fault might hurl him down into desperation, He said

Matt. vi.

1 Cor. ii. and iii.

Esai. xxix. c.

Acts xv.

Luke xxii.

[1] *Temerous*, rash, presumptuous.

The Tragedy

unto them, Satan goeth about to sift you like chaff and to undo and destroy you. Yea, you had been already utterly lost if I had not prayed for you, and for thee especially, Peter, by name, that thy faith should not fail, because thou wilt fall foulier than the rest, and I know that God hath heard my prayer. For although thou wilt deny me with thy mouth, yet thou wilt not deny me with thy heart. Thou wilt sin ; but sin shall not reign in thee, so that in thy heart thou shalt not yield to naughty temptations. I will suffer thee to have a foul fall, that by the means thereof thy temerous boldness may be bridled and rebuked. And again, that after, when thou shalt come to thyself and perceive thy own infirmity, thy heart shall be touched with compassion against those that shall sin, raising them up with knowledge, and confirming and boldening them with thine example. Now can I not perceive how it may be proved by the words before rehearsed, that Peter was Pope and could not err afterward, neither the Bishops of Rome after him according to his example.

MASSUCCIUS. We shall writhe all the words that ever Christ spake to Peter, to make for the Popeship of Rome. Let us writhe them also when Peter counselled Christ to forsake the cross, saying, Save thyself, O Lord.

LEPIDUS. What answer then made Christ?

MASSUCCIUS. He said unto him, Get thee out

The Tragedy

of my sight, Satan, thou troublest me; thou hast no perseverance of things belonging to God, but to man only. It is easy to prove that Peter was chief head of our Bishops of Rome, and they his successors, taking it of this fashion. But tell me on the disputation. I would fain hear the end of it.

LEPIDUS. This Ambassador of Constantinople would fain have brought other reasons forth and other sayings of Scripture against our Popeship; but the Emperor, moved by our bishop, willed him to hold his peace, and commanded the other ambassadors, that they should also say their minds. Then the Ambassador of Antioch spake in this wise :— *The Ambassador of Antioch.*

Because methinketh it sufficiently declared that Holy Scripture doth not only establish the primacy of Peter, but also seems quite contrary thereunto, I will speak my mind briefly as I am commanded; neither will I bring any more reasons or arguments than this one, although it be easy to find a number. Be it that we granted Peter to be the universal bishop ordained of Christ over His Church (which thing is not true), yet must it not therefore be granted that the Bishops of Rome ought to be Popes, but rather our Bishops of Antioch ought to be the chief and universal bishops. Because that our bishops and not the Bishop of Rome were the successors of Peter. For Peter was Bishop of Antioch, and so unlikely a thing it is that Peter was ever at Rome.

The Tragedy

To this argument Master Pseudologus made answer in the name of our Pope, crying out with a loud voice until his sides cracked again, saying, Peter was here our bishop in Rome twenty-five years together continually, and in this same city was he afterwards crucified.

Then the Ambassador answered, A pretty reward for pains taken in preaching. But tell me, I pray you, In what place of Scripture find you that he was ever at Rome?

Then answered Master Pseudologus, In no place of Scripture, quoth he. But it may well be found in our historiographers and in many other books of our bishops and other holy men. Whereunto the Ambassador answered, Then how know you by the Word of God that your Bishops of Rome be the chief universal Bishops of the Church of Christ, if ye have not that in Holy Scripture that Peter was ever at Rome? Truly if ye intend to prove your bishops to be Popes by the Word of God, ye must first prove by the same Word that Peter was ordained of Christ the universal head of His whole Church. And then must ye prove by the Word of God that Christ undoubtedly gave the same authority to Peter to make the Bishops of Rome after him chief bishops by continual succession; and, last of all, it must be proved by sure authority of the Word of God that Peter was at Rome, and bishop of

The Tragedy

the city, and died there. These things done, ye might well believe that your bishops were Popes by the Word of God. But there is not one of these three things that ye can prove by Scripture, especially the second and the third, as ye yourselves do confess. Wherefore I cannot see with what face ye can bear down so manifest a lie.

Then Master Pseudologus said, We know that our bishop is Pope, and that with a fulness of power; and we know that he hath received this authority of Christ by the means of Saint Peter and not of man. Wherefore we know him to be Pope by the law of God, and not by the law of man; and we will also hold and believe this truth as an article of our faith, notwithstanding that none of these things before rehearsed can be proved by the authority of Holy Scripture.

Then said the Ambassador—

Because we all be bound to believe the articles of our faith as the foundations and chief principles of our religion, it is needful that they appear most plainly by Scripture; and you will set fire and torments before the whole world to make men believe that thing which by your own confession cannot be proved by the authority of the Holy Scriptures. Where, I pray you, can men lay the foundation of their faith, if they be compelled to believe and confess as a necessary article of their faith, your bishop to be the universal head of the Church of Christ

The Tragedy

when there is not one word thereof in the Holy Scripture? It is an intolerable tyranny, the like whereof hath not been heard, to bind the conscience of men to receive so manifest a lie for an article of their faith, seeing it cannot only not be proved by God's Word, but also all the whole Scripture is against it. You ought to be content to bind men to believe that the Pope hath the highest authority of all. But ye will further compel them to believe that that power and authority cometh fully and wholly from God, and not from man, although that thing can in no wise be proved from Scripture. Furthermore, he would have it believed that it may be proved by Holy Scripture that our bishop was Pope, when you yourselves be forced to grant that it cannot be proved by Holy Scripture that Peter was ever at Rome. Of this chief and universal bishopric of your bishop ye can have none other opinion but that it is a device of man, seeing the contrary cannot be proved by the Word of God. And you will have it received for an article of the faith, and that it shall be believed with an heavenly faith. If ye be not sure whether Peter were ever at Rome or not, for the which cause ye challenge your bishop to be chief and the successor of Peter, how can ye have certain knowledge of this our chief bishopric, but upon the saying of men only, who naturally be liars?

The Tragedy

To this Master Pseudologus made answer: The men which said that Peter was at Rome were the chief bishops of all other, and therefore could they not lie when they so said. Wherefore we be sure and certain of our Popeship. Then the Ambassador said, Ye take for a ground that thing which ye had most need to prove, that is, that your bishops were chief bishops; and then, again, that they could not err; both the which points I utterly deny. If ye would say, Some saints affirm Peter some time to have been at Rome, I would straight make answer that I knew not whether they were saints or no, for that there is no word thereof in Scripture. But ye will peradventure say, They were canonised of our chief bishops which could not err; to that will I answer as before, that ye take that thing for your proof which remaineth first to be proved. Yea, and moreover will I say, Be it that ye were assured that they were saints, yet must it be granted that saints have sometime erred. And so it may be that they erred even the very same time when they said Peter was once at Rome. Namely, the thing being spoken of them not to that end that it should be received for an article of our faith necessary for salvation, as your mind is. Thus by all means be you in an error. But let us grant that there hath been some revelation touching this point, surely I must needs think that it was an illusion of the devil.

The Tragedy

Yea, be it that it were God Himself which had revealed the same thing unto you, and that it were truth indeed, and it was a revelation from God; yet because there is no word in all Scripture of the thing, neither have other men this revelation of yours, ye should in no wise force men to believe this your Popeship as an article of their faith. And furthermore, I will prove by strong reasons that these historiographers of yours, these bishops and saints, which wrote that Peter was the chief Bishop of Rome, and was put to death in the same city, lied unreasonably. And first of all tell me in good faith, What time say they that Peter was at Rome, and how long dwelt he there?

<small>That Peter was not at Rome.</small> Thereunto answered Pseudologus, that he came to Rome the second year of Claudius the Emperor, and was made bishop then, and dwelt there twenty-five years, by whose preaching Rome was brought to the faith of Christ, as both Eusebius and St. Jerome hath written.

Then answered the Ambassador, This is once plain (quoth he), that Christ suffered upon the cross the eighteenth year of Tiberius the Emperor, who reigned twenty-three years. After him succeeded Caius, and reigned four years. Then followed afterward, Claudius. Now then, if Peter came to Rome the second year of Claudius, ye must needs grant that Peter came to Rome within eleven years after Christ's death. Again, on the other

The Tragedy

side : it is plain by the words of Holy Scripture that Paul was not only not converted to the faith when Christ suffered upon the cross, but it appeareth also that he was not converted when Stephen was stoned ; because the Scripture is plain, that he kept their garments which stoned Stephen to death. This being so, Paul himself writeth to the Galatians that he came to Jerusalem seventeen years after he was converted, and that then he found Peter there. This was at the least the eighteenth year after the death of Christ. Then if Peter were yet at Jerusalem eighteen years after the death of Christ, how can it be that he came to Rome the second year of Claudius, as you say, which was the eleventh year after Christ's death ? You yourselves may easily perceive when ye say so, that ye speak directly against the manifest words of the Scripture. Furthermore, Peter was at Jerusalem not only eighteen years after the death of Christ, but the same time also he sent to preach the Gospel, not to the Romans, but to the Jews. And it is to be believed that he preached the Gospel amongst the Jews. And Paul also in the same epistle which he wrote to the Romans, because he saluteth a great many there by name, truly he would have saluted Peter also if he had been then the chief bishop there, as you contend. Wherefore it is easy to be proved that it is a very false lie that your historiographers do write. But, to say the truth,

[margin: Gala. ii.]
[margin: Romans xvi.]

The Tragedy

they that be named to write this gear be not the authors thereof, but they be your lies, which you have annexed maliciously to their books, directly repugning[1] to the manifest authority of the Holy Scripture.

Then Master Pseudologus brought forth a very old book that lay by him, so old that it was eaten with moths and worms, wherein there were certain epistles, I cannot tell what, written by Clement, as he said, whom he judged the first Bishop of Rome after Peter. In these letters, written by the same Clement to James, Bishop of Jerusalem, this thing was contained, how Peter, being at Rome and perceiving death draw near, in the presence of a number of Christian men, took Clement by the hand, and in the hearing of them all, said, Brethren, my death is now at hand, as Christ hath revealed unto me. Wherefore I ordain this Clement your bishop, unto whom only I deliver my seat, and the preaching of my doctrine; unto whom only I translate the same power of loosing and binding which I received of Christ. Then said Pseudologus, Lo! here may you see how that Peter was at Rome, and ordained Clement bishop after him, and set him in his seat, granting him his full authority.

Then the Ambassador would see and read those epistles, and when he had read and weighed them, he said, Master mine Pseudologus, ye cannot cloak your lies so craftily but they will appear

[1] *Repugning*, opposing or contrary to.

The Tragedy

as they be, that is to say, lies, even at the first sight. For these epistles of yours be nothing else but feignings of your own, without authority; full of vanities and lies. And that it is true, I say, hereby it might appear that even by your own historiographers Linus followed Peter, and not Clement. And after Linus followed Anacletus, and afterward Clement, who is numbered to be the fourth after Peter; and yet would you falsely place him to be the second. And moreover, by your own historiographers, if ye will account the course of the times as ye should, ye shall find that James was dead seven years before your Clement was bishop; wherefore I cannot say by what reason he could write to James, being dead. And again, even in the first beginning of the salutation he calleth him Bishop of Bishops, who should govern not only the Church of the Jews at Jerusalem, but also all other churches. And if James were then Pope, truly then was not Peter Pope, and therefore could not he make Clement Pope after him, neither, by Clement, his successors. And moreover, even by the same very words that ye allege that Peter should say to Clement before his death, it cannot be proved that Clement was ordained universal bishop of all churches, but only the Bishop of the Church of Rome. Besides this, if Clement was made Bishop of Rome by Peter, as you say he was, and not chosen of the people,

The Tragedy

no doubt his successors would have followed the same example, which thing they did not ; and therefore it is false that Peter made him bishop. I will pass over that neither Eusebius, neither Jerome, number these Epistles amongst Clement's works. Yea, and Clement himself in these epistles praiseth a book that he should write, the title whereof *Itinerarium Clementes*, which book, of truth, was never of his making. And furthermore, this book maketh mention of dioceses, archbishoprics, primacies, and bishoprics, which orders and names were not yet distincted[1] and appointed out ; neither doth he anything else in these Epistles but set forth the dignity and freedom of priests, whom he will have so free that they shall not intermeddle themselves with any handicraft, for a proof of the which absurdity he citeth certain places of Holy Scripture, writhed beyond the nock.[2] Moreover, in his second Epistle he is so bold to teach James of what sort he should minister the sacraments. And yet that fashion is not observed this day, namely, in the administration of the Lord's Supper. Furthermore, none of the ancient writers make any mention of these Epistles, neither yet of them that Anacletus or Euaristus should write. He citeth out of the New and Old Testament that it is not lawful for priests to sacrifice or sing mass, but

_{Distinct xv.}
_{Sancta Romana Eccles.}

---

[1] *Distincted*, marked off or distinguished.
[2] *Writhed beyond the nock*, strained beyond bounds or reason.

154

The Tragedy

when the bishop commandeth them; which thing can neither be found in the New, neither in the Old Testament. In the first Epistle he affirmeth that all things, wives and other, should be common, and that if it be not so, it cometh of the wickedness of men. There be also in the same Epistles many other foolish things and lies, which he rehearsed, but because ye may read them yourself, I will rehearse no more.

Master Pseudologus showed also certain other Epistles written, as he said, by Anacletus and Euaristus, whereby he minded to stablish this Popeship. But the Ambassador proved by good reasons that they were all of none authority, because that it is contained in them that Clement should be his predecessor, which thing Jerome denieth, and also Irenius. Further, he would not that priests should be accused or judged, for a proof whereof allegeth the Scriptures without judgment or reason. He will have bishops judges in secular matters, and that every man may appeal to them; when it is well known that that thing was never granted unto them before the time of Theodosius the Emperor. And again, he saith that Cephas signifieth a head, whereas, indeed, it signifieth a stone. And furthermore, I can prove the Epistles of Euaristus to be of none authority; not only by that he bringeth many sentences of Scripture safely writhed, that priests should not be

The Tragedy

accused of any laymen, but also because he writeth ad Gallium and Barduam, two councils in whose time Anacletus was Bishop of Rome, and not Euaristus, which thing is evident by the histories.

Master Pseudologus blushed, and was ashamed wonderfully when these things were laid to his charge, because he appeared openly to all men's sight to have played a false part; which thing when the Ambassador of Antioch perceived, he left him as he was, and gave place to the Ambassador of Jerusalem, who spake then wonderfully on this wise :—

The Ambassador of Jerusalem.

There is no doubt but that Christ, who was the chief and universal Bishop of His Church, preached His Gospel chiefly at Jerusalem, in the which place He was contented to die for our sakes. And this is also certain, that James succeeded in His room, who was next Bishop in Jerusalem after Christ. Wherefore if there should be any supreme, universal, and visible head, stablished in the earth, of the Church of Christ Militant (because it is sufficiently proved that Peter was not the chief bishop), our Bishops of Jerusalem ought to be Popes, and not the Bishops of Rome. For you would have your Bishops of Rome to be Popes, because of none other reason but that they succeeded Peter. We may much the better challenge our Bishops of Jerusalem to be chief bishops, because they succeeded Christ, insomuch as Christ is greater,

The Tragedy

and more excellent, than Peter. As touching Christ, it is known right well that He was the universal head of His Church, and that He was crucified in Jerusalem. And moreover, not only Paul nameth James first before Peter and John; but also in the first council of the apostles, whereas Peter, Paul, Barnabas, and the rest of the apostles speak, he, as their head and judge, said his mind last, which was approved of all the apostles and of the whole congregation. And it is not to be doubted but that if the Church of Jerusalem be the mother (as she is indeed) of all other churches, and of whom all other churches had their beginning, wherefore she ought to be called mother, as it was determined in Nicene Council; then must the Bishop of Jerusalem, as the spouse of the Church, be called the universal father of all churches and the chief bishop, and bishop over all other bishops, as your Clement calleth him in his first Epistle, if it be his as you do allege. Then thus he said: These words have I spoken, not that I think our bishops to be highest by any means (for Christ only is the universal head of His Church, who is only sufficient), but to declare unto you by a certain sure reason, if there must be any supreme head in earth, the same ought rather by right belong to our bishop, than to the Bishop of Rome. Ye may now see how much vanity there is in your reasons when our reasons be so slender and yet better than

Gala. ii.

The Tragedy

Gala. ii. yours. For Christ made neither Peter, neither James, the supreme head of His Church. And yet in the first council of the apostles, James said his mind last, as Bishop of Jerusalem, and Paul named him before Peter and John. But it followeth not therefore that he was universal bishop above all other bishops. Notwithstanding, this one thing is true, that our Church must be called the mother of all other churches; not that it ought to govern all other churches as you make your argument, which thing cannot be, but because all other churches had their original and first beginning of it. Wherefore our bishops have the first place in the council appointed unto them, and be called bishops of the first seat, because of the estimation of the city, wherein Christ was put to death. But they must not therefore be called the bishops of other bishops, and the universal heads of the Church of Christ.

The Ambassador of Alexandria. The Ambassador of Alexandria interrupted this Ambassador of his tale, saying, What need we so many words in so plain a matter? If the Bishops of Rome had received this authority at Christ's hand, that they should be chief bishops and governors of all other bishops, as you say, all churches and their bishops with them (the Church of Rome only excepted) had been from the death of Christ until this day ever styled heretics and schismatics, because they never acknowledged him to be their

158

The Tragedy

supreme head. And moreover, all councils which have been holden until this day should have been but devilish meetings, because they neither allowed, neither declared, the Bishop of Rome to be Christ's vicar, and the supreme head of His Church. But Nicene Council chiefly should have been devilish, not only because it gave not the first place to the Bishop of Rome, but the fourth; but also much more because they took so great and so heavenly a power away from him, the best part whereof they gave to our Bishop of Alexandria, who had the charge committed unto him of the churches in the East parts, unto whom he was appointed governor. And the Council of Africa should have passed all other in heresy, wherein it was established that the bishop of the first seat ought not to be called the Head Priest, Chief Bishop, neither by any such-like title, but chiefly because there was an ordinance made in express words that the Bishop of Rome by name must not be called the universal bishop. This is very certain, if the bishops received this monarchy of God, then were these councils devilish, which took this divine power away from them. Cyprian also should have been an heretic, not only because he calleth the Bishop of Rome, Brother, in his Epistles, which he wrote unto him, but much more because he maintaineth, with Saint Augustine, that there is none which is bishop of other bishops, and that it is a great tyranny to desire to be lord

The Tragedy

over other bishops. And also your Saint Gregory should not only not have been a saint, but also an extreme wicked and a condemned person; for he writeth expressly, that he which would be bishop of all other bishops, shall not have the place of Christ in earth, but of Lucifer, and shall be very Antichrist himself. And further, he bringeth in a number of inconveniences which should ensue, if the Bishop of Rome should take upon him the dignity of the chief bishop, as though it were by the law of God. Then thus he said, Seeing then that your primacy is not godly, nor of God, ye must of force grant that it is either of man or else of the devil. But it is not of man, as I will prove by strong reasons; wherefore it is of the devil. That it is not of man, this will I prove. The Emperor himself cannot give unto you any spiritual power. For you yourselves grant that this dignity which ye have, is not given you of the Emperor, but of Christ. Wherefore ye must acknowledge Christ to be your supreme head, as all other bishops doth, who confess not that they received this spiritual authority that they have, either of the Bishop of Rome, or else of the Emperor, but of Christ only. So that the Emperor cannot give unto you any dominion or power, saving that which is temporal, and that only in such countries as be under his governance. Seeing then he hath no dominion either in Asia or else in Africa, he

The Tragedy

cannot make you superiors to us ; neither have we any need to have you to be our governors, the princes that we have being sufficient for our tuition. He may give unto you some temporal power, but only in such provinces as be under him in Europe ; but he cannot give you the chief place, unless he will willingly forsake his Empire and set you in his place and make you above himself. Ye cry and say that ye be Christ's vicars. Truly, if ye be Christ's vicars, ye would endeavour yourselves earnestly to follow Him. When the Jews would have made Him a king, He fled and would not receive that dignity. But you be so far from following His example, whose vicars ye seem to be, that ye procured wonderful ambitiously this chief supreme dignity, contrary the express word of Christ ; who perceiving the apostles to contend which of them should be above other, He said unto them plainly, He would not have them strive to be lords and bear rule, as the princes of this world, but rather to serve. Christ Himself, as long as He was here in earth, would take no temporal dominion upon Him, that He might wholly be bent to the saving of souls, and that no let should hinder Him in setting forth the Gospel. But you, as though ye were superiors to Christ, will, like tyrants, with the offence of all the whole world, challenge unto you an universal dominion. Seeing then this primacy of yours is neither of God, neither

John vi. b.

Matt. xx. c.
Mark ix. d and x. e.
Luke ix. e and xx. b.
1 Peter v. a.
John xviii. e.
Matt. xx. d.

The Tragedy

of man, ye must needs grant that it is of the devil. Wherefore we all, as many as be here together, protest with one assent and voice, in the name of our churches, that we will not admit this primacy ; we allow it not, neither will grant we thereunto. But utterly and expressly we condemn it ; we will not obey it, but will withstand this unbridled tyranny of yours to the uttermost of our powers.

Then arose Master Gooplanus, a stout proctor of the Pope, and thus he began : Our chief bishop (quoth he) hath not taken this high dignity upon him to offend you, spoil you,[1] or to exercise any tyranny over you ; but only to defend you, to endue you with honour, and to profit you and to enrich you with benefices, titles, dignities, privileged immunities, benedictions, stations, absolutions, dispensations, pardons, suffrages, and jubilees, in the which things he will serve you all. He will be the servant of the servants of God, wherefore ye ought not to withstand him in a thing so profitable unto you.

To this the same Ambassador answered, saying, As long as ye cannot prove by unanswerable arguments that your bishop is equal with Christ, in spirit and love, we will never assent that he shall be our bishop and supreme head. If ye will have us to acknowledge him not only to be our chief bishop, but also our chief prince (as by your arguments ye appear to go about), and that we

[1] *Spoil*, despoil or rob.

The Tragedy

ought to believe that he may challenge unto him both the authorities, ecclesiastical and civil, ye must of necessity first show that he is above Christ in power, wisdom, and love, because it is well known that Christ would in no wise take upon Him any civil governance in this world. We be afraid of so monstrous and horrible a head. Wherefore we cannot allow this authority, neither that he should be our superior. If you intend to admit him, take heed ye be not too hasty, for ye shall perceive to your undoing, that he is no shepherd, but a bloody wolf.

Then arose Master Thrasibristus so suddenly, and so fiercely, that it appeared he could stay himself no longer. And being endued with a wonderful power, stoutness, violence, and fury, thus he said—

What need we have so many words for the defence of our Popeship, seeing that there hath been brought strong reasons enough to overcome the grossest wit in the world, insomuch that a blind man may see the truth of them? Wherefore because these our reasons, our pleasures, our gentleness, and fair promises cannot content them, our Most Holy Father must use his large and endless authority.

And then turning himself and speaking to the Pope, he said, You, Most Holy Father, be the supreme head of the Church of Christ, and there-

The Tragedy

fore be you above all other persons, men, angels, reasons, Holy Scriptures, authorities, yea, and above the whole world. There is no man may judge you, or else command you, for so it is come to pass. Now ye be Pope, and being Pope, ye cannot err. Therefore only say thus, We be Pope and we will be Pope; and it is enough. Your power and authority is so great, that if ye were not Pope, if yet ye once pronounced these words, We will be, ye should be, out of hand. Then looking upon the ambassadors with a fierce countenance, he said, If ye will be rebels to His Holiness, ye shall feel the lightnings and thunderbolts of his excommunications and cursings fly in the air, even to the furthest country in the East, and then shall ye know whether he be Pope or not. Moreover, we shall have Cæsar's help and favour joined to our strength; so that all we, coupled in one, will defend the Pope's authority with our sword.

Then all the ambassadors arose at once to answer this saying with one accord; but there was a sign made to the Pope's chaplain that he should do as he was bidden, and straightway he began with a loud voice the hymn *Te Deum Laudamus*; the noise whereof filled the air up to the stars, and all the rest followed them, crying, *Whow!*[1] Victoria,

---

[1] *Whow!* a shout of triumph, as our whoop, or hip before "hurrah," from the Middle English word *whowpen*, to shout.

The Tragedy

Victoria, Victoria! And even at the very same instant rang all the bells in Rome. The Pope himself was by-and-by caught with men's hands and borne upon their shoulders. And so they carried home the Most Holy Father to his place with a great pomp and triumph. Now must ye not marvel, though ye saw me, as ye said in the beginning, jocund and merry.

MASSUCCIUS. Alas! what became of the poor ambassadors?

LEPIDUS. They were all stricken in a dump by-and-by, and departed to their inns sad and heavy, taking this great rebuke so well as it might be.

MASSUCCIUS. If I had been in their coats, I would not have thought that it had been good tarrying for me then in Rome.

LEPIDUS. I think no man would use any violence against them.

MASSUCCIUS. Well, I am sure the Pope would no more send them wine of Greece and Corsica.

LEPIDUS. Or if he sent any, it should peradventure be mingled. But now can I tarry no longer with you, for now I see the night draweth on, and I have an exceeding deal of business to do. Think ye not, where this disputation was? Even where there was none else by, saving the Pope's most faithful friends, who would say nothing but that should make for the Pope.

MASSUCCIUS. If it be as you say, either will

The Tragedy

they hold their peace, or else they have very little to say to their commendation.

LEPIDUS. Ye be in a manifest error. For there was never so great a lie, but it may be so craftily coloured and painted, that the blind common people may think it very true. I have now told you all the whole matter, desiring you to keep it secret as ye promised me at the beginning.

MASSUCCIUS. I will do the best I can; but methinketh it will be very hard for me so to do. I thank you heartily for your pains for showing this pretty story so fully and so diligently.

VI

LUCIFER AND BEELZEBUB

LUCIFER. I have thought good to call you again together here in this place, that I might rejoice with you for the birth of Antichrist, so happy and so unlooked for; even as the angels rejoiced in Christ's nativity. But now must we lay our heads together, and take counsel by what means and device we may establish this our kingdom and increase it, and bring it to the highest degree of all wickedness and mischief. Methinketh it were best first to go about so to set forth and amplify his honour, that men by little and little may take this Antichrist for a certain God in earth, and honour and magnify him even as their God. That we may use the high authority which he hath, for a handsome and strong instrument to the committing of all kinds of deceits, mischiefs, and wickedness, we will prime in men's hearts (inasmuch as in us lieth) that Christ gave the keys of the kingdom of Heaven to Peter and his successors, and also full power and jurisdiction, not only of

The Tragedy

the empire of this world, but also of the heavenly kingdom.

BEELZEBUB. Truly this thing pleaseth us very well, so that he have none authority in Hell over us, for we be surely persuaded that he will come to so high a degree in abomination and wickedness, that if he should have the rule over us but one day, he would bring us into a great deal worse case than we be.

LUCIFER. It is even as thou sayest. But we will foresee to this jeopardy wisely enough, for my trust is to bring him to such a wickedness that he shall adventure with his thievish fingers to corrupt the Holy Scriptures, and shall violently and mischievously writhe them to the establishing, increasing, and exercising of his intolerable tyranny. I know well they will not be ashamed to say, when Christ said to Peter, Thou shalt be called Cephas, that He meant, Thou shalt be called Head, and so was Peter made head of all the apostles, who willingly obeyed that primacy; and also that Peter afterward left this chief high authority to the Bishops of Rome by succession.

BEELZEBUB. If the matter would come thus to pass, in case Peter should be raised again from death, he should no more be Pope; no, he should have no manner of authority.

LUCIFER. Indeed he should have no more than should please our Bishop of Rome to grant him of

The Tragedy

his bountiful liberality. And this thing is very notable: we will cause all their lies to be written in their canons, and so will we blind the eyes of the unlearned that they shall take the same canons for things most holy. And also we shall all cause the Church of Rome, notwithstanding it is most wicked and heretical, that it shall not only be accounted for the Church of Christ, but also it shall be taken for the head and mother of all other churches.

BEELZEBUB. Surely the Churches of Christ will never so take it, though our churches so do.

LUCIFER. Yes. Men shall have this opinion of the Church of Rome chiefly, and so of all other churches that shall hang upon her, that they be the Churches of Christ, though they be ours never so much. We will persuade also that the Church of Rome is without spot, and worthy to be as a glass and example to all other churches.

BEELZEBUB. Yea, of all abomination.

LUCIFER. All shall follow after her, as after a chief lady mistress that cannot do amiss, who hath full power; unto whom all may appeal, and from whom none may appeal; unto whom men must run for refuge in matters of weight, as it were to God, because she may be judge to all other, and be judged of none other, and may call again her sentences as oft as her listeth, and change statutes made in councils, and pronounce him an heretic

The Tragedy

which dareth speak one word against it whose seat, dignity, and authority is highest, by the which authority she may gather general councils together, and by whom all doctrines shall be allowed or disallowed; who only may determine and stablish controversies in religion of what matter so ever they began; who only may expound the old canons and the Holy Scriptures as it pleaseth her; and that all men may know and obey her, though the thing she command seem never so wrongful and intolerable. Now if the Church of Rome have once so large authority, and yet be under the Pope, even as the wife is in the subjection of her husband, consider then with yourselves how great authority our high Bishop of Rome shall have. For besides all these things rehearsed, he may bring to pass that the sentence which he hath once given and allowed for good may be vain and of none effect. He only shall have authority to establish new religions; and all such ordinances as he shall make must be received with no less reverence than though they had been spoken with God's own mouth. Because that his goodness shall be the health of men, and may have none other judge but God alone; and that it is not necessary that he should purge himself of his fault when he is accused by other. Because Peter hath left to all Bishops of Rome by continual succession, not only all his merits, but also his innocency, and because

The Tragedy

he hath authority over justice. And also because his power is of God, and the Emperor's of the Pope, and hath authority full, and whole, in earth to appoint and determine what him listeth in all controversies that come in question in matters of religion ; for he hath the solutions of all controversies hid within his breast, and he is the heir of all the empire, and of the kingdom of the Romans ; and therefore may he do what he will, for he hath as much authority as ever had Peter.

BEELZEBUB. This only thing excepted, that he cannot raise dead men to life again, as Peter once did.

LUCIFER. He only hath authority to canonise saints ; he only is above all councils and ordinances ; he only may dispense against justice, and he only may change God's definitive sentence. And if it were so that all the whole world should speak against the Pope, yet must the mind of the Pope only be allowed. He only hath knowledge of the Church, and that after such a sort that he only can change the nature of things and make somewhat of nothing. In him only must the will only be esteemed, for the best reason that can be devised, not so hardy that any man should say unto him, Why do you this, or this thing, after this or that fashion ? For he can make righteousness of wrong, and amend all things as he shall think good ; he can expound and change laws, and make

The Tragedy

all square things round, as one that is neither pure God, neither pure man.

BEELZEBUB. Then shall he be a devil, or else some kind of brute beast. But I think it no very hard thing to persuade all this gear to him, his mind is so wonderfully puffed up with ambition. Yet can I not see how men may be made believe that the Pope is their God in earth.

LUCIFER. Yea, ye know not that it is an easy thing to deceive the common sort of the unlearned, particularly[1] in matters of religion. You know right well that they be naturally inclining to all kinds of superstition. There is none so shameful a lie, nor no deceit so far out of frame, that the whole world will not readily receive, if it be delivered them by any authority with some colour and likelihood of a truth. What Christian man is he which will not willingly believe that Christ is ascended up into Heaven, and hath left His vicar here in earth endued and furnished with a full power and authority to do all manner of things ; at the leastwise that faults might be amended, which amongst a number of matters readily arise in the Church by the reason of His absence ; and that especially when the world hath conceived a wonderful good opinion of their life and learning which shall be the setters forth of the matter ?' And moreover, we will accurse him, whatsoever he

[1] In the text *namely*.

The Tragedy

be, and declare him an apostate, a blasphemer against the Holy Ghost, irregular, worthy to be suspended and degraded, that will adventure to speak but one word against our Popehood. And if it fortune that he be a bishop or a priest that commit this fault, we will have him declared excommunicate, delivered into the power of Satan, an heretic, a defamed person, an infidel, a committer of sacrilege, a schismatic, a damned and a cursed body. Who is that will not be afraid of these words when the very sound of them, being spoken, is so fearful? If these threatenings will not be sufficient, then indeed will we attempt most cruel persecutions; men shall be cast in prison and shall lose both life and goods. There shall be no fault in the world more heinously punished than this one of disobedience against our Popehood. Men shall hear God blasphemed, and some deny the might of God, and some mock God, and yet shall all men laugh and make a game thereat, as though it were but a trifling matter. But if any man shall attempt to deny the Pope's power, or to diminish the same never so little, he shall be burned alive with long torment. Moreover, we will cause all the books to be burned, as many as shall seem to make anything against our Popehood. Yea, and we will forbid men that they shall not have the Scripture in their hands, nor in their sight, under the pain of fire and rope.

The Tragedy

BEELZEBUB. This thing would they do very gladly, because the Scriptures be against them. But it would be so manifest and open sacrilege and wickedness that it cannot well be cloaked, with no colour, pretence, fraud, or craft. Truly it shall be enough to corrupt the Scriptures, and violently to writhe it to their crooked purpose, without all fear or shame.

LUCIFER. They shall not allow nor suffer any books to be read but such as maintain this craft and falsehood; so that even as the simple sheep follow their shepherd, so shall the Christian men their heads; and we will so endeavour ourselves to blind men, that they shall not only believe and magnify this high bishop for their private commodity, but they shall also defend it tooth and nail, even to the very death.

BEELZEBUB. But how may it be brought to pass that they shall not see so manifest a lie, they being the heads of the Church?

LUCIFER. We will juggle their eyes with proud titles, high dignities, offices, and benefices, the revenues of whom shall be fat stipends, that they may make gauds and triumphs with all abundance of pleasure. We will also make laws that the people shall not only reverence them, but shall also esteem them as gods for their religious and popish holiness; and again, that men shall alway study and occupy all their wits in their heads to preserve

The Tragedy

and increase this dignity, whereunto there may appear some hope that they shall attain. All shall hang upon the Pope's sleeve ; not for fear only of loss of their office, benefices, yearly revenues, and promotions, but also upon hope to get more. Now may you easily judge whether they will apply the powers of their strength and wit or not for the setting forth and establishing of our Popehood ; and the earnester they will be in this point, the more necessary and profitable a thing it will be to them to defend the same. For if the Popeship once fall, they should all starve for hunger, because they have none honest craft or exercise to take them to. Yea, and I will cause the Pope to forbid them all honest kinds of exercises, and that under a colour of religion and holiness ; lest peradventure the hands and consciences of spiritual men should be fouled[1] with labouring, they shall all be occupied (such shall be the boasting) about the health of souls. So great shall they be that they shall disdain to preach God's Word ; neither shall they be otherwise occupied than in celebrating again and again their cold and superstitious ceremonies, and that with such a pomp and glory that it shall be a showing and a setting forth of themselves.

BEELZEBUB. In what kind of exercise, then, shall they occupy themselves all their lifetime, for it is a very painful thing to be always idle?

[1] *Fouled*, from the Middle English verb *fŭulen*, to defile or soil.

The Tragedy

LUCIFER. They shall not be always idle, good sir, but shall have something ado always, in dicing, carding, banqueting; in wantonness, contention, and other such-like courtly pastimes. And that they may be more diligent in the maintaining of this Popeship, I will provide for them, under a pretence of an ecclesiastical law, that they shall be disburdened and free from all exactions of princes of this world. Moreover, I will make a law whereunto shall be sworn all bishops and doctors that they shall not only attempt nothing against this Popehood, but shall also maintain and defend it to the uttermost of their power. And also for the establishment of our Antichrist, it shall be stablished by a law that these wicked wretches, moved thereunto by our spirit, shall sometime congregate themselves together in their wicked councils only to keep down and extinguish (by a common consent) the truth of the Gospel. By means of the which congregation they shall retain all the princes and magistrates of the earth to confirm their tyranny, and to defend this detestable abomination of the Pope. And we will make the world believe that such councils cannot err; which thing will be easy to compass, men shall be so blind and ignorant. We will also devise for the Pope's pleasure a new kind of divinity altogether vain, superstitious, void of learning, heretical and wicked, full of vanities and darkness, of man's inventions, doubts, questions,

The Tragedy

and contentions; the mother of all sects, errors, and abominations. This evil kind of divinity shall bring in such a darkness that it shall hurt and deceive very good wits. There shall be no school, neither university, which shall not be hurt and infected with this Antichrist of ours. Good letters shall be banished, and so shall they lack all good learning, insomuch that their children (though they be baptized and therefore dedicated to God) they shall learn nothing else in their schools but vain and filthy tales. And furthermore, that the tyranny of this bishop's empire may be the more strongly and surely established, the Popes, being inspired with our spirit, shall write decrees and decretals, that is to say, profane, wicked, and abominable sentences. And yet, notwithstanding, the world shall be in such a blindness that they shall think them very holy decrees. And to conclude in few words, though God only be to be worshipped and prayed unto with a true, loving entireness of mind; yet by my crafts will I bring it to pass that the Pope shall command men to pray, not only to angels and saints and to such as were most wicked, and yet by him canonised, but also unto their images, pictures, and relics, and that with as stinking a kind of superstition as may be.

BEELZEBUB. Verily I cannot perceive, how ever it will come to pass that Christian men may fall into so manifest vices, wickedness, and idolatry.

The Tragedy

Of a truth, if there would come such a time wherein these detestable vices might be committed that ye have now spoken of, I think the Christian men would have more idols than ever had either the Jews or the Gentiles, and would exceed with their wickedness and idolatry all other nations of the world.

LUCIFER. But I promise you that we may easily bring it to pass by the means of this our head, that men shall fall both into these and all other kinds of abominations. If ye doubt how this thing may be brought to pass, I will tell you, that ye may help to set it forward to the uttermost of your powers. It is not unknown unto you that they have a custom in the Church of Christ, when any Christian man suffereth martyrdom, the rest of the Christian congregation doth what they can to have their bodies honourably buried, as it is a thing both honest and godly. And their bishops verily upon the same day that those martyrs suffered, be wont to make mention of their constancy and victory; to the intent that men should be encouraged not only to follow the example of the saints, that they may be strong to die for the glory of Christ, if the thing so require, but also for a witness of the resurrection that is to come, and to bring men in a contempt of this life, which shortly will fade and perish, into the hope of life everlasting; which devotion God hath sundry times approved and confirmed with sundry miracles. Now will we move and stir men under

The Tragedy

a pretence of religion and holiness to rip and cut up their dead bodies, and to put their bones in vessels of crystal, silver, or gold, and to set them upon altars, where the Lord's Supper is accustomed to be ministered, as in a place most holy and replenished with all godly religion. In the mean space the people shall flock thither together, and shall begin not only to pray to the saints, but also to their bones and relics. Which idolatry we will confirm with some miracle of ours, by the same power that God hath permitted unto us, as He promised in Holy Scriptures. Of this shall arise such superstition amongst men, and such an unadvised zeal of religion, that by-and-by they shall begin to build temples, chapels, and altars, which shall be hallowed in the honour of these saints, and there shall the images of them be set forth to be seen of the people. Yea, and verily shall their feasts be kept, that even as a great number of the Jews ran to Bethania,[1] not for Jesus' sake only, but to see Lazarus when they heard tell that he was raised again by Christ from death, so shall Christian men run to the churches, rather for to see and worship those images and relics of saints, than for Christ. Neither is it to be doubted but that a time will come when they shall set more store in very deed by saints than by God, although they will peradventure be afraid to

[1] Bethany.

The Tragedy

say so. And also we must handle the Pope wisely, whom they shall take for their god, that he may not only allow these mischiefs and abominations, but that he may of himself will them and command them. This thing will he do, not only for the gain and private commodity that shall arise thereof, when he shall see people run to dead men's bodies, to images of saints, to altars and pictures, and offer there much money, build gorgeous and sumptuous chapels and churches, and give unto them great yearly revenues, whereby his kingdom shall be increased ; but also for the opinion of religion and holiness, that he may show himself as a god in earth, and able daily to find out new religions and fashions that were never seen before, neither known to men that be alive, neither to the old holy fathers, neither yet to Christ Himself. Then as tyrants be accustomed to do when they will reign, which make common games and triumphs and goodly shows, wherewith to occupy men's minds, that the people gazing upon the sights present shall have no leisure to fancy how to avoid the tyranny, or to consider how to discharge their shoulders from the burden of bondage, so shall the Pope of a like sort judge it meet to devise daily new rules, new religions, new kinds of serving God, new trades of living, and new ceremonies. Thus shall he do, that men being taken and astonished with marvelling at these news, and fast tied

The Tragedy

with the rope of superstition and blinded with the enchantment of error, shall have neither leisure, neither means, to open their eyes, whereby to espy out the Pope's abominable wickedness.

BEELZEBUB. All this gear pleaseth us very well, one thing only excepted.

LUCIFER. What is that one thing that pleaseth you not?

BEELZEBUB. Notwithstanding that there can no greater abomination be committed than that ye have rehearsed, yet will he now be much worse than we. Wherefore I fear me lest when he shall die, and come down hither to Hell, that as he passeth us in wickedness, so he will be above us in dignity.

LUCIFER. Know ye not that as Christ for His humbleness was announced above all the companies of angels, so also must Antichrist for his pride be announced above all the orders of devils? We must take this service well and worthy. And as for my part, surely I would not stick to lease my chief rule in Hell, of condition I might wreak my malice upon God. Think ye that he will desire to be anything else over us than our head, as he is in the world, the head of our members? But, I pray you, suffer me to make an end of my matter. Ye know right well that the chosen of God be saved by the mere mercy and goodness of God through Christ, who is dead for them upon the

The Tragedy

cross; yea, and that the good things which either they have now, or had in times past, or hereafter shall have, all came of the pure grace and tender mercy of God by the death of Christ, whilst they believe in heart and mind, and assuredly feel in the spirit, that all these things be given them of God freely; in the which things consisteth the true Christian religion. But I, by the means of our head, will praise and magnify by little and little the light of nature as much as may be, and that man hath of himself, his wit, his wisdom, his power, his freewill; and in the mean space will I minish[1] the law of God; I will bury Christ, and shadow the grace of God with darkness so wittily and so warily that men shall believe that they be able (as they shall dream) to fulfil the whole law of God by a certain influence of His grace granted to all men; and, moreover, to do certain other works of much more perfection than those works which Christ commanded, which works they shall call works of supererogation. By the means of these works shall be established sundry new fashions of living, and new rules shall arise which shall be allowed by our chief bishop, although they be plain contrary to the law of God, to Christ, to the grace of God, and to the Gospel. And the professors of these rules, studying under

[1] *Minish*, diminish, from Middle English verb minyshen, to make small or lessen.

The Tragedy

a pretence and shadow of great holiness and perfectness of religion to amplify the dignity of the chief bishop and commending it above the moon,[1] as blind leaders of the blind, shall first deceive themselves, and afterwards almost the whole universal world. These new monstrous creatures shall preach; these shall be believed, when they shall cry that the law of God is imperfect, and that their fathers have fulfilled that which was of God omitted, and have joined many perfections to the law of God not disclosed to the world as yet, neither by the prophets, neither by Christ, neither by the apostles, without the keeping of the which things men cannot be perfect. Furthermore, they shall affirm and contend that men shall receive the grace of God by this most holy and strong thing called Free-will; and that they may, by the help thereof, keep the law of God and fulfil His commandments, full and whole; and besides these works which God hath commanded, that they be able to do other works of more perfection. And they shall hold that men may make recompense sufficient to the goodness of God for all the gifts which either they have received or shall receive at His hand, how much soever it be that they have received; and that they can satisfy for all the sins whichever they have or shall commit, and for

---

[1] *Above the moon*, beyond reason. In pictures of the Assumption of the Virgin, the moon is represented as a crescent under her feet.

The Tragedy

what thing else soever it be that they be bound to God for; and that they may of themselves deserve all manner of goods, bodily or ghostly, which either they have or shall receive of God. So that they shall imagine themselves able to deserve so much glory that God is not able to repay and reward the thing that He oweth unto them. And therefore shall they sell their merits to other men as though they had superfluous, and too many. And because they can never sell or give so many but that they shall always have a number remaining, they shall make our Holy Father the Pope the inheritor of their merits, that he may accomplish all things for all men requisite. And this rich treasurer of merits he shall sell wonderful dearly in his jubilees and pardons; and so fond an opinion shall they have that they shall think themselves able to deserve God's free election, and shall think God's heavenly providence and all things that belong to salvation to hang upon their freewill, and upon their Pope.

BEELZEBUB. If it be so as ye say, then is Freewill a great lord and shall be above God Himself. For, as I perceive, he shall either choose or refuse health or condemnation like a lord, and God, as his servant, shall minister occasions and time convenient unto him. So shall the will of God be like a bondwoman, and the will of man like unto a queen. It shall be necessary not that man

The Tragedy

shall apply his will to God's will, but that God shall apply His will to man's will; neither can God choose men without the Pope's licence. So that in case God had never so reproved and rejected any man, and the Pope (in whose hands all power is) mindeth to save the same man, God's determination shall be void. And so shall the Pope be greater than Christ, and man's freewill also, because the whole salvation of all mankind shall be in their own power. But Christ, answering the children of Zebedee, of whom the one desired to sit on the right hand, and the other on the left, said it was not in Him to give that thing, because all hung upon God's free election, and Christ also said not true when He so said, for He should have granted that all depended upon the Pope, and man's freewill.

LUCIFER. If he were not such a one, he should not be Antichrist. And because the election of God doth abase a man and casteth him down more than anything else; which thing man, being naturally inclined to esteem highly himself, cannot abide; therefore shall it be an easy thing to persuade to men that all the whole matter hangeth upon his own freewill and not upon God. Therefore will the Pope never forsake this office, to promote and further this our purpose by all the means that he can, and that for many other causes; but chiefly, for that man's merits shall be as it

The Tragedy

were a groundwork of all his merchandise, and vantage. Howbeit, that he may better sell and utter them, he shall mingle some merits of Christ amongst them, and shall boast that he hath the key of all these treasures, and full authority to distribute, to apply, to sell, and to give all at his will and pleasure. And also a time shall come when the world shall believe (because they shall think him a God in earth endued with most great authority) that he can both bind and loose, save or condemn, when it shall be his pleasure. Now may ye easily perceive whether men will run to him or not, to buy Heaven and Paradise of him. Oh! how many and how abominable fantasies shall men commit, when they shall say to themselves, What care I? Of this I am sure, that I shall be absolved for money. What a number of souls shall be damned, thinking to be saved by their own merits, by the Pope's pardons and absolutions, because they shall be without faith and without Christ! Out of this devilish fountain shall spring jubilees, stations,[1] pardons, absolutions, dispensations, relaxations, and an infinite number of monsters which daily shall they devise to sell; Christ and His merits; and Heaven and Paradise with all. Furthermore, we will cause that this our mischievous parricide shall by his fraud and craft persuade Christian men that Christ with all His

[1] *Stations*, offices, posts, and grades of rank.

The Tragedy

merits, passion, death and benefits be not sufficient to save, I will not say the reproved and rejected sort, but even the very chosen of God, be it that they believe in Christ with never so lively a faith. For they must, moreover, of necessity confess all their sins both open and private, even the very inward thoughts and desires, yea, and all the branches and circumstances of them, and disclose all things, whether they be spoken or not, to a priest of him appointed.

BEELZEBUB. This thing is not possible to be done, for their sins be innumerable.

LUCIFER. Surely our priests cannot devise a better way to hold men's consciences in a perplexity, doubtful and uncertain. And so when men shall be in a continual doubting whether they be in the favour of God or not, they shall run oft to our priest, and his gain shall always increase, in that he shall receive well for his absolutions.

BEELZEBUB. If there should such a time come, when I might see Christian men disclosing their secrets, even such as be of greatest weight, and that, slandering themselves contrary both to the law of God and the law of nature, and oftentimes also with no small offence of their neighbour, to a wicked thief; and should also suffer their wives, their daughters and sisters to open the bottom of their hearts, and matters of no honesty, not always to a fit man, but most commonly to a vicious varlet,

The Tragedy

I would be bold to say they were the most fools in the universal world. But tell me in good faith, what profit should ensue of this devilish foolishness if it should be brought into our Church?

LUCIFER.[1] Oh, it should much increase and amplify the honour of our bishop and his members, and be a very great gain and profit to his Church. For then should men believe that he, by his ministers, did pardon sins, and not God, and that the same sins were not forgiven by the virtue of the passion of Christ, but by the virtue of the absolution that they heard the priest speak. And in confession, mention shall be made of all things saving of Christ, and so shall we bury Christ together with His passion and death, and God with His grace. And moreover, what a great commodity shall it be to the Pope, trow you, when his ministers by this means shall know all the secrets of princes? I pass over how that in hearing of women secretly disclose their dishonesty, with all the circumstances thereof, and all unhonest thoughts and desires, such confessors, being inflamed with the communication, and considering craftily how their minds be inclined, will begin many fair and handsome snares (which they may easily make) whereby to hold them, even as it were by the hair of the head, when they are once

---

[1] In the text this speech is put into the mouth of Beelzebub; but I think this certainly must be a typographical error.

The Tragedy

made privy to their secrets. And ye may furthermore guess that priests will not give their labour in absolving for *God have mercy;* but will rather sell it for no small sum of money. And they shall also require them to do the penance that they have enjoined them; which thing shall make much for their commodity, and also profit not a little to their Holy Church of Rome. And this thing also shall be without doubt, that the Pope, being desireful of part of the gain, shall reserve many matters and offences, from the which no man may be absolved, but at Rome, of the Pope himself, or else of his confessors appointed there, so that money must walk largely.

BEELZEBUB. There be also many silly old wives, which have breaths that savour not all the best. I marvel how the confessors shall tarry to hear the reckoning of all their faults.

LUCIFER. They shall despatch such quickly with two or three words, without tarriance in searching out the bowels and bottom of every vice, as they shall do with the younger women.

BEELZEBUB. And how, I pray you, may we bring it to pass that this confession may be used among men?

LUCIFER. Ye know well that Christian men which be troubled in conscience, be straight wont to run to some learned man for counsel, how they may have lively faith, and be increased and estab-

The Tragedy

lished in the same, how they may take heed to themselves from sin and be perfect, whom the said learned men absolve; that is, they show them by God's Word that they be absolved if they believe in Christ; and so he giveth them counsel, and showeth them the light of truth. Ye know also that such as be excommunicated be wont after repentance to come to the priest, and show him that they be sorry for their offences; who, perceiving that it is true, absolveth them, and doth notify to the whole congregation, that they be absolved and amended, by the means whereof they shall be received of all men as brethren. Then do they enjoin them penance for their public offences which they have committed; not that they can satisfy in the sight of God by that penance, before whose throne Christ hath made sufficient satisfaction, but to be an example to others, that neither they nor any other commit the like any more. These will be good and handsome beginnings, whereby to bring in by little and little our confession. For we will persuade men that the priest must know their consciences that they may be absolved of their sins. And then will they tell all their offences both open and secret; yea, and they will believe that they be absolved, not by Christ, but *per opus operatum*, that is, by the work that is wrought by confessing; that is to say—for the remembering of their sins, for the shame where-

The Tragedy

with they be touched in telling their sins, for the contrition, for the absolution of the priest, for the penance to them enjoined, and for the Pope's pardons. Neither need you to doubt whether the bishop will be content with this confession, for he will gladly command it to all Christian men ; and that it may be the more esteemed, he shall boast and lie that he received it of Christ, with such a commendation that he ought to be burned which denieth it to be of the law of God. But this thing I would not have unknown to you, that such men as be oppressed with tyranny, they be delivered by death from all bondage and servitude if they be not delivered before. But as for the poor Christians, though they die, yet can they not by any means avoid the tyranny of our Pope, for at that time especially they be snared, that is to say, in the hour of death, and be taken prisoners in a place (where or what it is I cannot tell) named Purgatory. This Purgatory shall be builded by our Pope full of flame and fire, whereof he only shall have the keys, out of which place no man can get unless the Pope license him, and yet[1] paying a sum of money, whereof shall so much gain arise, that the profit of that only shall be more unto him than of all the rest of his promotions and benefices.

BEELZEBUB. And who is that shall come into

[1] *Yet*, moreover or besides.

The Tragedy

this Purgatory of theirs, they which die in faith, or out of faith?

LUCIFER. They that die in faith, for all the other be ours without Purgatory.

BEELZEBUB. Then is not God with His grace enough for such, neither Christ with His life, passion, and death, neither the help of so many saints, neither his own merits or confession, nor contrition, nor satisfaction, nor absolution, nor all the penance in the world, neither jubilees, neither yet pardons.

LUCIFER. In this our confused kingdom of Babylon all things must be doubtful and uncertain.

BEELZEBUB. What! our faith in Christ also?

LUCIFER. That shall be altogether doubtful, for this shall they take as a chief article of their faith, that every man ought to doubt of himself whether they be chosen or not; whether God hate them or favour them; whether Christ died for them or not; yea, and though He died for them never so, yet whether He satisfied for their sins or not.

BEELZEBUB. And how can they establish this Purgatory of theirs?

LUCIFER. Our word shall be their ground.

BEELZEBUB. How?

LUCIFER. I will show you. When you shall obsess[1] any man, and their priests and friars come with their conjuring to conjure you, ye shall say

---

[1] *Obsess*, possess, or enter as a familiar spirit into a man.

The Tragedy

that ye be the soul of some of their acquaintance, which died long agone, and remain to this day in a place full of flames and fire, that they call Purgatory, where you must remain until their sin be clean purged, and that ye shall soon be delivered if they will procure a certain number of masses to be said for you, and if they once promise you to do so, then ye will for a testimony of the matter, trouble no more the party so obsessed, which thing ye shall perform if it be promised. Then when men shall perceive it to be a matter in good earnest they shall think it be so indeed. And priests and monks shall favour much the matter, for the great gains that they shall have thereby. Yea, and they shall so favour it that in continuance of time it shall be made an article of faith, though it be a thing most wicked. And they shall be rewarded with faggot and fire that will adventure to speak one word against it. And also they shall persuade the unlearned that this fond[1] flameless fire of Purgatory may be proved by the Holy Scriptures. And here likewise shall the Pope's authority be required that it may be stretched out to Purgatory.

BEELZEBUB. Methought I heard you speak of masses. What things they be I cannot tell. Wherefore my desire is to know what kinds of creatures these masses be?

[1] *Fond*, foolish.

The Tragedy

LUCIFER. Truly, of other things that belong to the Pope's dominion, the mass is both most holy and most pestilent. In the outward show and shining and beauty it shall be most holy; but yet in deed most pestilent. Ye know right well that the Lord's Supper was instituted of Christ in the remembrance of His passion, and being distributed, as it should be, in low and apostolical simplicity, was a thing, and is to this day, that hath brought much comfort and consolation to the chosen of God. But now our Holy Father shall not only change the substances of it, but also change the accidents of it in the mass. So that the Supper of the Lord shall no more be the Supper of the Lord, neither in substance, neither in fashion, neither in likelihood, neither in show; but it shall be altogether contrary and enemy to itself, and full of wickedness and superstition. For whereas the Lord's Supper was first ordained of Christ to call again the passion of Christ to the remembrance of the faithful, they, to blot out that exceeding great benefit of Christ, shall boast that they offer Christ again to His Father in their masses, not for the quick only, but also for the dead. As though they should say: When Christ offered Himself once upon the cross to His Father, He made not satisfaction sufficiently enough for the sins of all mankind; wherefore we offer Him again daily, and nail Him again upon the cross, desiring the saints to help

The Tragedy

Him, to make His oblation perfect. And whereas Christ in the institution of His Supper appointed bread and wine—whose example His ministers should follow, teaching what thing it is and to what end, as Christ did, and exhorting together that they should lift up their minds into Heaven, being stirred by this heavenly sacrament, that they should have their eye set upon Christ only, and so by faith to use Him for a heavenly food of their souls—they, to announce their dignity and authority, and to cause themselves to be accounted gods in earth, shall persuade men falsely, that liberty to minister that sacrament is only granted to the anointed, shaven, and oiled priests of the Pope; that the Supper of the Lord shall be translated, by that head of abomination the Pope, into the mass. And they shall boast that these fat massmongers, with pronouncing certain words (what they be I cannot tell) as it were in an enchantment, have not only by-and-by consecrated, but also transformed and transubstantiated, the bread into the Body and the wine into the Blood of Christ. This will they do, not only to increase their estimation, but also that men being deceived by eating that Host, although they be without faith, shall think they possess Christ's clothes, hair, and all. Yea, they shall bring men into the belief, that by the only hearing of one of these masses, or seeing the Host lifted up, most plentiful grace and pardon,

The Tragedy

as they call it, shall be granted. And like arrant thieves, they shall rob the laity of the cup, that is to say, of one-half of the Supper, against the express word of God, to declare that they be more worthy men and in higher authority, and that there is a great difference between the common people and the Pope's anointed. They only shall be fed in their private masses whom they shall not be ashamed to sell for money. And they shall keep the bread so by them consecrate in a box, as it were in a prison, and that shall they set forth to the people to be worshipped as a god. And they shall not only carry it about in their pomps and open shows, but it shall go before the Pope as though it were his footman. To be short, though the Lord's Supper be a thing most holy, yet being changed into the mass, it shall be a thing most pestilent. Moreover, the Supper, which was ordained of Christ to be unto all Christian men as a pledge of His promise, peace and concord, the same, being once abused, shall be the original and well-spring of all discord, dissension, contention, heresies and sects, for the diverse and sundry opinions that men shall have of the same sacrament. We will also make a law that these priests anointed by the Pope shall have no wives.

BEELZEBUB. Why, I pray you?

LUCIFER. That they may appear outwardly altogether heavenly and celestial like angels, so

The Tragedy

that therefore men shall marvel more at them, and set the more store by them; yea, and moreover, that the Pope and not their children may be their inheritors; but chiefly that they may be without the troubles that chance in matrimony, and being at liberty under this colour, may commit all kinds of filthiness that ever was done in all the world.

BEELZEBUB. Think you that they will condemn marriage?

LUCIFER. They shall say it is a wicked thing. And although it be agreeable to nature, ordained of God, confirmed of Christ, yet shall they forbid it to their nuns, monks, and priests, and to all their other creatures. Yea, and at certain times they shall forbid it to all men, and in certain degrees that they themselves have devised, that by the means thereof they may get a great sum of money for dispensations. And at certain times they shall forbid wholesome meat to be eaten, which God hath created to be used to His glory, and to be taken with thanksgiving. At certain times of the year he shall not suffer them to eat but once in the day. But all these things shall notwithstanding be dispensed with all for money. He shall make of this sort an infinite number of other precepts which he will say be necessary to salvation. And so in making new articles of the faith, he shall wander through all heresies which by man's judgment and wisdom have a certain

The Tragedy

likelihood to set forth God's glory more worthily. And to comprehend this large matter in few words: I will apply all the powers of my wit that this creature of ours may do much more hurt to the souls of men than Christ Himself did good. And it is not to be doubted but that we will make of this Church a very Babylon. True it is that a thing of such holiness cannot be brought in a moment suddenly to the highest degree of abomination; wherefore in this noble mischief we must go forward by little and little, letting none occasion slip and opportunity of time shall offer unto us. Now therefore shall you have my licence to depart, requiring you to lose no time.

BEELZEBUB. We will do your commandment.

VII

MICHAEL, GABRIEL, CHRIST

CHRIST. Mine angels, see you not how a mortal man in earth, being most vicious and abomination itself, with no small injury and contempt of God, adventureth to settle himself in the Holy Place, and to boast himself to be my vicar and the universal head of my Church? See you not how under that pretence he hath crucified me again and buried me again with all my great benefits, my gospel and my grace? See you not how he hath defiled and infected the Holy Church, my well-beloved spouse, whom I myself have redeemed, washed, and cleansed with mine own proper blood?

MICHAEL. We see altogether and marvel truly very much how ye could suffer (now about four hundred years) such horrible abominations.

CHRIST. Although the judgments of God be for the most part hid from the knowledge of human creatures, yet must they be taken as they be indeed, to be righteous and holy. For the

The Tragedy

will of God, as it is most right, of necessity it is not only impossible that it should err itself, but also it is a rule of all other wills, and therefore must every creature take it for best reason. And yet one cause can I bring why God would suffer so much evil to reign so long space.

MICHAEL. We take the wickedness of man to have deserved these great mischiefs, and that so it ought to be, that God should suffer them so to fall, as they have fallen, into so great evil, darkness, heresies, and mischiefs; because they loved not Thee as they ought, Thou being the chief light, truth, wisdom, life, and righteousness; neither would they obey Thy word.

CHRIST. There be many causes why God hath so suffered this long space; but the chief is that He would make His glory more notable. And you know that during the reign of this Antichrist not one of the elect have perished. Seeing they be in the hands of me and my Heavenly Father, none shall take them from me, neither can any of them perish. And ye know also that this wicked abomination with all his malice, crafts, fraud, subtleties, errors, deceits, proditions,[1] offences, evil examples, mischiefs, promises, flatterings, rewards, threatenings, slanders, persecutions, torments, and deaths, have not hurt any whit in any one point the soul of any one of my chosen. But their

[1] *Proditions*, treacheries.

The Tragedy

malice hath rather made mine more glorious, in that their virtue hath been tried as gold in the furnace; and those that be false Christians by this proof be declared to be hypocrites. And therefore, whether he will or not, I have used him as an instrument and a servant for the larger setting forth of God's glory. And moreover, God would have all the devils of Hell and all evil men, to abuse this head of theirs to the destruction of my kingdom by deceit and violence, that I being moved by that occasion should withstand, overcome, and destroy this head of abomination, and triumph worthily of him, as ye shall shortly see; by the which victory I might set forth more clearly the power and wisdom of God. Mark, therefore, now, and ye shall see, how that in destroying of him, that he may be destroyed with more ignominy, I will not use my power, but the bare words of my ministers, whereby I will disclose these great mischiefs, and will lighten their minds with the knowledge of the truth. I know that men will then open their eyes; and when they shall perceive that they have been so long time buried in such darkness of ignorance, in that they have worshipped abomination itself instead of God, they will humble themselves under the strong hand of God, and shall know what a miserable creature man is, and what he can do when he is destitute of God; into how many

The Tragedy

dangers he falleth headlong, and how necessary a thing the grace of God is for him. Now be all mischiefs and abominations come even to the highest state and degree that they can come; the measure is full, their wickedness exceedeth and is spread over all. Therefore must I no longer suffer. For, as I have promised, I must and will shorten these woeful days of malice for the love of my chosen. I must disclose this wicked head of this abomination to his confusion and God's glory. For, as I have said before, there is nothing hidden but must be revealed. Ye shall see that when, as I took manhood upon me, and appeared visible into the world, although sin reigned, stirred up by the law, and ruled all with a great force and power, yet I in dying upon the cross had the victory, and overcame valiantly all the enemies of God; even so now will I triumph of this shameless and wicked head of abomination. First and foremost, I will destroy the tyrannical dominion which he has wrongfully used in the simple consciences of men; and afterward will I take away from him his temporal power. And to his further rebuke, even as the world hath taken him for a god in earth this long space, so will I now cause the world to acknowledge him to be the most wicked tyrant that ever was or ever shall be amongst men. You, mine angels, that be appointed to the ministry of my chosen, ye shall do your duties diligently.

Matt. xxiiii.
Matt. x.

The Tragedy

And to thee, Gabriel, as thou wast sent to Daniel to tell him the time of the coming of Messias, and afterwards also to Zachary, to signify unto him the coming of my forerunner, John the Baptist, and last of all to my mother, to declare unto her my conception; so shalt thou now go to Henry the Eighth, King of England, in whose heart thou shalt print and persuade that, all delays set apart, he drive this cruel tyrant out of all his realms and dominions. Dan. ix. *e.*
and x. *e.*

Luke i.

GABRIEL. Forth we will gladly, O Lord, and with a swiftness of spirit perform your commandment.

CHRIST. Ye shall understand that Henry the Eighth shall deliver his dominions from the tyranny of this mischievous robber; and he shall not utterly cleanse it from idolatry and superstition, whose roots be further entered into the hearts of men than that they can be pulled out again at the first pluck. For he shall not long live after this valiant enterprise attempted. But I will give him a son, named Edward the Sixth; and because he shall be one even after my own heart, endued with sundry godly gifts, as one that shall love me unfeignedly, and shall perceive how many and diverse ways he is bound to God, he shall not abide this great and rank enemy of mine. Therefore following his father's steps he shall purge all his kingdoms and dominions from all

The Tragedy

the superstition and idolatry of Antichrist. I will be always with him ; neither shall he want of my favour, grace, and defence at any time, and he shall have a Christian Protector whom I will use as a means and instrument and very fit messenger betwixt me and the king to perform this my purpose, whom I will give unto a very valiant man, both in nobleness and in uprightness of mind, and a singular lover and friend of right religion ; by whose wisdom and gravity I will have mine Edward to be instructed and brought up even from his childhood, that all the days of his life he may have continual war with all things that shall displease God. This chosen instrument of mine shall be the first that shall bend his spear against the forenamed, mine unpardonable enemy, whose wonderful example, most worthy to be followed of all others, the rest of the princes of Christendom shall be astonished to behold, and shall apply themselves to follow his enterprise, being encouraged by his worthy virtue. Neither shall it be needful for him to use any violence whereby to purge his kingdoms of these mischiefs, lies, heresies, superstitions, simonies, idolatries, wickednesses, and betraying of souls, wherewith the whole world was replenished by the means of this abominable thief. For all these things, though they be very heinous, shall vanish away suddenly, and be brought to nothing at the coming of the

The Tragedy

light of my Word, which he shall always use as a continual burning light, both in this and all other his doings. Happy therefore shall you Englishmen be in that ye shall frame all your affairs earnestly to God's glory, to the salvation of His chosen elects and my worthy triumph.

MICHAEL. So shall it be.

VIII

HENRY THE EIGHTH, PAPISTA, THOMAS, ARCHBISHOP OF CANTERBURY

HENRY VIII. We have sent for you into our presence, as for men which have more knowledge in the Scriptures and old writers than the rest of our realm, to resolve us of a doubt that is come to our mind. Therefore two things we require of you, the one that every[1] of you say his mind frankly and freely, what he thinketh, without respect of favour or displeasure to any man living ; and the other that ye keep it secret and disclose not one word of the things that shall be here reasoned. For it is a matter of great weight, and toucheth our honour ; wherefore we charge you so long to keep counsel until the truth be known, and that you have licence of us to open it. There is a thought entered into our head which we be persuaded cometh of God :—That the Pope, who heretofore hath been taken for a god in earth, is very Antichrist, and if we had certain knowledge

[1] *Every*, each one.

The Tragedy

that this thing were true, we would, as we are bound, banish him out of all the coasts of our kingdom, not only because he should no more rob us of our treasure, but much rather lest he should any longer exercise tyranny in men's consciences and bring such a number of souls in danger of everlasting damnation. If he were the vicar of Christ indeed, we would be his loving children from henceforth, as we have been in times past. Say now every of you, your minds soberly and truly what he thinketh.

PAPISTA. I cannot but marvel very much when I hear your princely Majesty make a doubt and questioning of matters that be most clear, questionless, and certain. I cannot perceive that it is lawful to think, much less to speak, of such a matter without doing God open wrong. For such holy things as the Popehood is, ought to be worshipped and not doubted upon and called in question.

HENRY. A truth, if it be a truth, the diligentlier it is discussed and examined, the clearer, the brighter, and more plain it appeareth. Therefore when we dispute of this matter, truth hath no wrong, but rather a benefit. Therefore if the Pope be indeed Christ's vicar in earth, the more seriously this truth is reasoned of, the more plentifully shall it be published abroad, and all men shall more gladly and readily receive it. So that

The Tragedy

we will neither do the Pope wrong, neither the truth, but shall rather show them both a singular pleasure. And it is not to be doubted but that heavenly things must be worshipped. But now here is the question, Whether the Popeship be a heavenly thing or not? and this is the matter which we desire to have discussed.

PAPISTA. Peradventure your Majesty doth mind to accuse all our forefathers, all kingdoms, and all Christian men of heresy, by whose judgment the Pope hath always been, and is to this day, taken of Christ's vicar in earth.

HENRY. That the truth cometh to light is not the cause that maketh men heretics, but rather delivereth them from all error, deceit, heresy, and betraying. And truly we desire nothing else than to have the truth bolted forth by all means possible. In the end of our disputation, if we shall be assured that the Pope is Christ's vicar, we will so take him as we have done hitherto, and we shall be much more strengthened in that opinion without hurt of any creature. But if we shall perceive the contrary, and be assured that he is Antichrist indeed, then surely will we endeavour ourselves to rid us from his tyranny wherein we have lived hitherto, taking him to be a certain god in earth. And also all other errors and incommodities must be taken away which spring out of this counterfeit belief; and moreover, we will endeavour ourselves to rid

The Tragedy

other men also from the same. So that I see not what can come of this disputation, but that shall be good and godly.

PAPISTA. Truly we might worthily be noted of a temerous[1] arrogancy, if we should think ourselves able to know and judge better than a number almost infinite of worthy men both in religion and doctrine, who without all question believed the popeship to be a heavenly thing. And moreover, what opinion shall we conceive of an innumerable sort of Christian men, which either now be, or else hath been, in times past, and have died in this faith, or live therein this day? Surely in so weighty a matter it behoveth us to leave off disputing, and fall to believing.

HENRY. If such as believed that the popeship was an heavenly thing were deceived, it is plain that they were neither learned nor holy in that point. And therefore ought we in a matter of so great importance to open our eyes, and be wiser than they. As for the blind multitude, I think must not be followed, who receiveth that manifest error for an article of faith; but if such as believed that the Pope was Christ's vicar in earth were not deceived, but being in this opinion thought well, surely we will take them both for learned and holy. We mind not this by our disputation to take from them one jot either of their wisdom or

---

[1] *Temerous*, rash, imprudent.

The Tragedy

holiness; but we shall be rather confirmed and strengthened in the same good opinion which we have conceived, both of them and of the popeship. If our intent be to overcome them with the light and knowledge of the truth to God's glory, putting not our trust in our own strength, but in the only goodness of God, our godly study must not be called a temerous boldness. Neither do I allow the saying that we ought simply to believe it. That is to say, grossly, for then should the Turks and heretics be excused. But as Paul saith, We must prove all, and take only that is good.

PAPISTA. Surely, as for my part, I cannot persuade myself in my conscience that I may put my tongue in heaven, and dispute of the popeship, as though I doubted of so great a matter.

HENRY. Your divines be not afraid to put their mouths and tongues both in heaven, and to dispute in their schools and books, whether God be or not. And the same thing dare your preachers also, even in the pulpit; though there be none that doubteth of so manifest a truth; and yet standeth it not with your consciences to reason in a brief disputation of the Bishop of Rome's primacy. May it ever come to pass or not that the Pope shall be so much greater and higher than God, that it shall not be lawful to speak of his primacy, and lawful enough to dispute boldly of God's essence?

The Tragedy

PAPISTA. It is lawful to dispute whether God be or not, without any remorse of conscience and without danger, because the reasons which be brought for the contrary part be so weak, and the other so strong, clear, and pithy, whereby it is proved that God is, that after such disputation men remain much more assured. But there cannot be a disputation of the primacy of the Bishop of Rome without pricking of conscience, because this thing is not so clear and evident as the other is; that is to say, that there is a God. And perhaps if it should come in question, we should remain in greater doubt than we were before. Wherefore it should seem that it were better to let the matter sleep as it is, and not to question thereof.

HENRY. Then you yourselves grant that the popeship is a doubtful thing, and again on the other side ye would have us shut our eyes, and believe it and embrace it, and undoubtedly to receive it for an heavenly thing. If the popeship were a thing indifferent, which could neither hurt nor profit the soul of man, it should seem no matter, though we left reasoning thereof, and let it remain quiet as it is without disputation. But forasmuch as upon the Bishop of Rome hangeth our salvation, if he be Christ's vicar in earth, as they say he is; and again if he be not, upon him contrariwise hangeth our damnation,

The Tragedy

we have determined to know the truth of the thing. And so much the more desirous be we to have this disputation go forward, for that we see you so earnest to refuse the same. We may be well assured that we shall offend God in no point of this disputation if we do all things soberly, with a meek spirit to the glory of God, having always God's Word for our judge, which is the only and everlasting rule of truth.

PAPISTA. Because it seemeth good to your Majesty that it be so, I, for my part, have nothing else to say; but that the Bishop of Rome is Christ's vicar in earth with full power.

HENRY. We know not whether he be Christ's vicar or not, but to the intent to have a perfect knowledge thereof, I have sent for you. Of this we be well assured, that the most part of them were exceeding vicious; we perceive also that the great ecclesiastical revenues which of right belong to the poorer sort of Christ be by him consumed and sold for ready money, and the cure of souls also, whom the Son of God Himself redeemed with the price of His blood. And they be not afraid to commit so weighty a charge (even the cure of souls) to the children which be evil born and worse brought up, and to men unlearned, wicked, and vicious. We also know that he doth not only sell his privileges, relaxations, compositions, and dispensations, but his jubilees also; his pardons

The Tragedy

and remissions of sins, his absolutions, his blessings, his masses, his burials, his sacraments, yea, and the merits and blood of Christ, and heaven itself. And it is well known that they have carried away great treasures out of our kingdoms, we receiving nothing again but ink, and parchment, and seals of lead. Under pretence of their buildings and wars against the infidels they have polled more money from us than all our kingdoms be worth. A blind man may see what means they use to rob both quick and dead, insomuch that of the House of God they have made a den of thieves. And all these things have they done under a shadow of religion and a pretence of holiness. If a man could open his eyes, and look upon the discords and strifes which they have sown in all Christendom, and see the blood they have shed, the slanders and offences they have committed, the souls they have lost, and the vicious life of them that will be called most holy, who ought to jeopard their own lives to profit their neighbour. If (I say) he could see how they be covered with fraud, unfaithfulness, and deceit, how they trouble all the whole world with such thunderings in contentions, as though heaven and earth went together, and all for none other cause but to increase their yearly revenues, to preserve their falsely pretended honour and their vain titles; surely he would not judge them to be the vicars of Christ, but rather

The Tragedy

to occupy the room of the great devil of hell.

PAPISTA. Be it that their works were never so wicked, yet cease they not therefore to be Christ's vicars if their doctrine be sound.

HENRY. Yea, marry, that is the thing that we be desirous to know, whether he be Christ's vicar or not; whether he be Antichrist or not; whether his doctrine be true or false; whether we ought to worship him, or to banish him out of our kingdom. Therefore of these things we be desirous to hear other men's minds.

THOMAS, ARCH. When God determined to save His elects, first He disclosed Himself by a certain light showed in the Old Testament, by His prophets and holy men before He came into the world, and He minded so to do not only because He would be known afar off that men should put their trust in Him and so be saved; but also that at His coming He might be known again by the same signs and tokens, and the gentlier received; of a like sort when He determined for the larger setting forth of His glory to publish the triumph of Christ, and the perfect and happy state of His elects, He painted forth and expressed lively in the Holy Scriptures that such as have unworthily the name of Christians must have one head in earth, full of abominations and wickedness, to the intent that he, being dis-

The Tragedy

closed unto us, we should not only not give credit unto him, but should by all means possible shun his wicked tyranny. First, therefore, as touching the place, God hath plainly declared unto us that he must be born at Rome. As Daniel the prophet wrote, who described the four monarchs of the world under a similitude of four beasts, that is to say, the Empire of Babylon, which was of the Assyrians, the Empire of the Persians, of the Grecians and of the Romans. And out of the head of the fourth beast (that is to say), out of the head of the monarchy of Rome, sprang a little horn (that is to say), Antichrist himself; who hath so announced his might and power that he hath broken the power both of the other horns and also of the Empire of Rome, and hath prevailed against the godly. The same thing Paul the Apostle confirmeth, saying, Before Antichrist be revealed and appear very strong, there must be a departing or going away, that is to say, the people must fall away or depart from the obedience of the Empire of Rome, as all holy men take it; wherefore of necessity it must be granted that he must have his seat at Rome, for he shall succeed the Emperor of Rome. Moreover John, in his Apocalypse, setting forth the Church of Rome unto us to be, not the spouse of Christ, but of Antichrist, saith that he saw a certain whore, the mother of all uncleanness and abomination of all

The place of Antichrist's reign.

Dan. vii.

2 Thess. *a* ii.

Apoc. xviii.

The Tragedy

the world, gorgeously arrayed with gold and stone, holding a cup of gold in her hand, with whose mingled liquor all the dwellers of the earth should be made drunk, from the highest to the lowest. And further this whore shall be made drunk with the blood of saints and of the martyrs of Christ. And upon her forehead she had written Babylon. And lest any man should doubt whether John spake of Rome or not, he saith plainly that the whore sat upon seven hills, which thing is well known to be agreeable to Rome, whereupon it is called the City of Seven Hills. Wherefore his seat must be at Rome; which thing is evident both by Holy Scripture and also by Jerome in an epistle that he wrote to Fabiola against Jovinian to Marcella, to Algasia, in the forty-seventh chapter of his Commentaries upon Esay, and in the second chapter of Osee.[1] The same thing is confirmed by the authority of Tertullian, writing against the Jews and the Gentiles in a book of the Resurrection of the Body, and of St. Augustine also in his books *De Civitate Dei*. In the same opinion also is Nicholas de Lyra upon Daniel and many others besides. And if we will weigh Paul's words diligently we shall also know the time wherein Antichrist must be disclosed to the world. For, writing to the Thessalonians, that thought Christ should shortly come to judgment, and

Apoc. xvii.

The time of Antichrist's disclosing.

[1] *Osee*, Hosea.

The Tragedy

minding to bring them out of that opinion, saith that there shall be a departing come before the Day of Judgment. That is to say, that men must fall from the empire of Rome, as Jerome, Anselm, Theophilact, Bede, Dionise, and almost all the rest of the interpreters take it. True it is that Paul spake this thing darkly, lest he should offend men's minds. Therefore then (saith Paul) that great wicked body shall show forth himself. Yea, and he shall not only succeed especially at Rome in his own strength, but also, as Daniel writeth, he shall destroy and bring to nothing the rest of the horns and strength of the empire of Rome. So that we now see plainly enough that the people hath not only shrunk from the obedience of the Emperor of Rome, but also that the emperors have had no dominion in Rome more than this seven hundred year. The bishops have occupied the place in the stead of the emperors, by the which bishops chiefly the emperors' power hath been minished. Wherefore we must grant that they be right Antichrist. Besides this, Christ Himself hath expressed and painted forth Antichrist and all his qualities in Holy Scriptures with so lively colours that whoso seeth the Pope and hath never so little light of knowledge, and seeth his properties, cannot choose but he must also know that he is very Antichrist. And to speak somewhat of him generally: Even as Christ is the

margin: 2 Thess. ii.

margin: Dan. vii.

margin: The properties and qualities of Antichrist.

The Tragedy

head of all His elects, so shall Antichrist be the head of all them that be rejected of God, which be falsely named Christians. As in Christ all trea-
<small>Ephes. iii.</small> sures of knowledge and wisdom of God be hidden, so in Antichrist shall be hidden with a cover of
<small>Colos. ii.</small> hypocrisy all mischiefs, crafts and deceits, guiles and falseness, which be in the great devil of hell himself. And, moreover, as the Holy Ghost is given to Christ, and poured into Him without measure, and not hemmed in without any bounds
<small>John i.</small> or limits, and as Christ is full of grace and truth,
<small>Colos. i.</small> yea, in Him dwelleth all fulness of perfect virtue and perfection, so there dwelleth in Antichrist all vices, wickedness, abominations, deceits, and lies without all measure. So that as Christ is the very true and lively image of God, so shall Antichrist be the very true and lively image of the devil. Where-
<small>Esay xi.</small> fore Esay calleth him the Wicked One. David
<small>Psalm x.</small> also writeth him to be the head of all wickedness.
<small>Dan. ix.</small> Daniel and Christ Himself call him abomination
<small>2 Thess. a ii.</small> itself. Paul calleth him the wicked man, the child of perdition, not only because he shall be lost himself, but because he shall also destroy all them that shall follow his steps and doctrine.
<small>1 John ii.</small> And also Saint John called him Antichrist, that is to say, a contrary enemy and a repugning adversary to Christ. And because he especially above all other creatures shall show himself to be an enemy and an adversary to Christ, therefore in that his

The Tragedy

exceeding contrariousness against Christ, he is called Antichrist. Now as Christ was conceived of the Holy Ghost and born of the Virgin Mary, so shall Antichrist be conceived of the spirit of the devil, and born of simony and ambition, which shall be in the minds of them that shall declare him Pope. Then shall the Pope be created of the most corrupt and infected congregation of people that is, whom they call cardinals; who, as though they were the very pillars of mischief, shall sustain all the world and all the wickedness thereof upon their shoulders. They say this order was created of God when He said, The pillars of the earth be of the Lord, and upon them He laid the foundation of the world. Hereby it is easy to be seen whether they understand rightly the Holy Scriptures, or else writhe them violently to their crooked purpose. Whoso shall read their histories and will diligently consider by what craft, hypocrisy, and dissimulation, fair promises, gifts, deceits, and proditions, and such like wicked means they have achieved to this popeship which they so much desired, he shall easily perceive of what spirit they were both conceived and begotten. Yea, they have given themselves wholly to the devil, so that they might once come to the popeship, as it is plainly written of Sylvester the Second.[1] He that

---

[1] This Pope is reputed to have had recourse to sorcery and other magical practices.

The Tragedy

could see by what spirit the popeship was conceived in the minds of men and appeared to the world should soon know whether it be a thing of God, or of man, or of the devil. Four hundred and fourscore years after the birth of Christ, that little horn of Daniel, that is to say, the Bishop of Rome, had but little strength and power of man, because they had none authority but only in their own dioceses, as other bishops have. But about the year of our Lord 480, Odoacer reigning in Rome, it chanced that Achatius, Bishop of Constantinople (who then was placed first among the bishops, and yet used no authority over them), would have condemned Peter, the Bishop of Alexandria, of heresy. And because the Bishop of Rome, for the worthiness of the city, was then in some estimation, the Bishop of Constantinople wrote to Simplicius, then being Bishop of Rome, desiring him that he would likewise declare the Bishop of Alexandria an heretic. And of this hath ambitious fellows taken occasions (unworthily, God He knoweth) to dispute of the authority of the Bishop of Rome. And so far have they gone forward in their ambition that they have not been ashamed falsely to contend that they are the heads of all other Churches. And on the other side stood they which took parts with the Bishop of Constantinople, affirming their bishop and not the Bishop of Rome to be the supreme head of all

The Tragedy

other Churches. This ambitious contention continued amongst these most holy fathers a hundred and twelve years; and at the last, about the year of our Lord five hundred, when Maurice the Emperor was in Greece, John, the Bishop of Constantinople gathered all the bishops of Greece together at Constantinople, and there was the Bishop of Constantinople, and not the Bishop of Rome, ordained of them to be the bishop of all other Churches. But when Maurice willed the Bishop of Rome to submit himself and his Church to the Bishop of Constantinople, Gregory, who then was Bishop of Rome, withstood it, and called him a forerunner of Antichrist. And the same Gregory, writing to the Bishop of Antioch and Alexandria, amongst all other things, saith, Ye know that in the Council of Chalcedon the title of the universal bishop was offered to the Bishop of Rome, which he would in nowise receive; neither was there any of our predecessors that did usurp that title. Yea, even then (as they say), to confound and rebuke the pride of other, he began to be named the servant of the servants of God. Howbeit his successor, Boniface the Third, a man too ambitious and crafty, obtained of Phocas the Emperor by subtle trayne[1] the dignity of a Pope.

---

[1] *Trayne*, stratagem, deceit; from the Middle English verb *trayen*, to betray. Treason and betrayal have the same source. The Latin form is *tradere*, to surrender.

The Tragedy

What manner of man this Phocas the Emperor was it appeareth of his history. By violence, fraud, and treason he came to the empire, and caused Maurice the Emperor, most cruelly and most wickedly, and his wife and all his children, to be killed before his own face. This was the holy man who first gave this goodly creature of the popeship to the world. And this is true that until the days of Constantine, the fourth emperor, the Bishop of Rome was wont to be confirmed of the Emperor. Howbeit at the request and entreaty of Benet the Second, of Rome, the foresaid Constantine granted to this Benet and his successors that they should be received and taken of all men for popes without the Emperor's confirmation. And so by little and little they crept up so high by their crafty diligence that the Emperor must both be confirmed and crowned of the Pope; but yet it is necessary that first he take an oath that he will defend the popehood. Therefore it is not hard to be known what manner of spirit it was that brought the popeship into the world, and how the creation of the Pope and of the popeship is contrary to the birth of Christ; namely[1] when, as Paul writeth, Christ glorified not Himself, neither thrust Himself to be a bishop, but taking example of Aaron, He tarried until He was called of His Father. But these men thrust

[1] *Namely*, particularly.

The Tragedy

themselves in violently until they have made themselves not only equal with Christ, but also above Christ. Christ, being in the shape of God, did cast down Himself willingly, and would take the shape of a servant upon Him. But this fellow, being in the form of a man which is a most abject and vile sinner, so proudly hath announced himself aloft that he is not ashamed to brag himself to be a high light and a god in earth. And if we will consider and weigh the life, the manners, and the works of Christ and the Pope, we shall find them altogether quite contrary the one to the other. Christ was innocent, poor, and would not trouble Himself with worldly businesses, but was altogether bent to the health of souls, whom He desired to enrich with heavenly treasure. He was meek, gentle, refusing both crown and kingdom; never had He any private affection of favour either towards Himself or others, His kinsfolk or towards any man living; being inflamed with a great force of the heavenly spirit, always sought He the glory of God the Father Eternal. He was a peacemaker, sober, subject to all men for the honour of His Father; merciful and very prone and ready to be pitiful. And therefore He wept upon Jerusalem. He was godly, shamefast,[1] chaste, most liberal, full of love and all other virtues. But all the popes be in all points diverse and quite contrary to

---

[1] *Shamefast*, modest, retiring.

The Tragedy

all these virtues of Christ. For there is a rotten dunghill and puddle within them of all uncleanness, wickedness, and mischief, as it is right well known to them that have any knowledge of them that be nowadays, and read the histories and lives of them that be past. And although they be very contrary to Christ in these things that I have spoken of more than other men be, that is to say, in all outward action of virtue, yet in their doctrine, and certain other their wicked abominations, they be most wicked and most contrary of all. For there be certain wickednesses peculiar unto them which be of exceeding great weight, and be so heinous that they be meet for none other but for these thieves only. Wherefore it is very necessary to grant them only to be the very and chief Antichrists, for these only be they who corrupt the Scripture, and, notwithstanding the express word of God, have plucked Christ with their wicked hands out of His high and glorious seat; and yet, not being contented with that horrible mischief, they have cast down, oppressed, and buried, and have banished quite out of the eyes[1] and memories of man the Redeemer of all mankind, and have placed themselves in Christ's seat, giving to themselves, and with force challenging[2] like tyrants, all that dignity which pertaineth to Christ

---

[1] *Out of the eyes*, out of the sight.
[2] *Challenging*, demanding as a right, or laying claim to.

The Tragedy

alone. Yea, they have made themselves above Christ. So that in conclusion they would not only seem equal to God, but also have announced themselves with a devilish and intolerable boldness above God. That this thing is as I say, it is evident. For the body of Christ's Church hath but one head ; otherwise it should be a monstrous deformed thing, the like whereof hath not been heard of ; and should not be a body knit together with a true proportion of the members. But Christ is the true and only head of His Church, and Paul doth plainly write that out of this head is the spirit, life, light, and righteousness poured into all the other members of the chosen. For He is our life, light, and righteousness. Now, on the other side, the Pope saith :—I am the head of the Church militant. If ye will have light and knowledge of heavenly things, ye must come to me, for I only am above all learned and holy men ; above the councils and above Holy Scripture itself ; yea, and also above your faith. Wherefore ye must believe according to my word ; and although the words of Holy Scripture be the words of God, yet must they be expounded and declared after my fashion, and as I say. I am only he which cannot err. Wherefore as concerning matters of faith, every man ought to shut his eyes and trust to my word, and stick thereunto undoubtedly. The Pope saith, moreover, If any man be dead

Ephes. iiii.

John xiiii.
John viii.
1 Cor. i.

The Tragedy

in the sight of God and a sinner, let him come to me; and out of hand, by the help of my absolutions and pardons, he shall live, and be made righteous in the sight of God. As though he should say, I am your light and righteousness, and not Christ. What thing doth pull Christ violently out of His place and thrust in himself, if this do not? Christ is our chief and everlasting priest, as it is written of Him; who, when He had once offered Himself upon the cross found out everlasting redemption for us, and satisfied for our sins, and pleased[1] the wrath of God, the Father, for ever. The Pope saith, I am the chief Bishop of the Church of Christ; the sacrifice that Christ made was not sufficient to satisfy for sin, and pacify the wrath of God. And therefore have I ordained the sacrifice of the mass and other offerings and meritorious work. To do thus is not only to pluck Christ out of His place and put in himself, but it is also a manifest confession that Christ was an imperfect priest; because that with His sacrifice He made not sufficient satisfaction for our sins, neither pacified the wrath of God enough, and therefore hath He need of the Pope's help; yea, and it is also a confession that the Holy Ghost in Holy Scripture was a liar, which thing is nothing else

_{Psalm cix.}
_{Hebrews v. and x.}

---

[1] *Pleased.* I am inclined to think that this is a typographical error for *peased*, from a Middle English word *peasen*, signifying to appease or pacify. Or it may be *pleased* in the sense of *satisfied*.

The Tragedy

but a mind to place himself above God. For the Pope can neither lie, neither err, in matters of faith, and God did both lie and err by His confession. Christ also is the only mediator between God and man, as it is written, No man cometh to the Father but by this mediator. He is the way and the gate that leadeth to God ; He is our advocate, our propitiation, our holiness, our redemption and health. He only is our Jesus and Saviour, neither is our salvation in any other but in Him only, as Peter writeth. And therefore Christ calleth all men unto Him, saying, Come to me, all ye that labour and be burdened with the burden of sin, and I will give rest and quietness unto you. Whoso thirsteth for salvation, let him come to me, and he shall be refreshed. But the Pope contrariwise saith, I am he, by whom ye may pacify the wrath of God ; by me only and by my ministers ye may obtain remission of your sins. I am the way that leadeth to heaven ; I have the keys of the kingdom of heaven ; I can open and shut at my pleasure to whom, when, and after what sort it shall please me. By me only ye may have life everlasting, and God will be merciful and pleased with you. Neither will I that ye shall have Christ alone your mediator and advocate in heaven ; but I will that ye choose some amongst them that be dead, such as like you best, so that they be canonised by me, and take them for your mediators, inter-

1 Timothy.
John xiv.
1 John ii.
1 Cor. i.

Acts. iiii.

Matt. vi.
John vii.

The Tragedy

cessors, proctors, advocates, and patrons. I will also that ye seek for your salvation, not in Christ alone (though Peter say plainly that it can be found in no other) but chiefly in me, in my absolutions, benedictions, and pardons, and in your own works also, and in the merits and intercession of saints. Wherefore come to me, all that be troubled with sorrow of conscience, and in me ye shall find peace.

Now whether all these things be most cruel, wicked, and blasphemous or not, he may easily perceive that is not altogether blind. Therefore it is most true that Daniel said, speaking of him, that he should be such a shameless blasphemer that he should speak against God Himself. And we also know that, according to the doctrine of Paul, every Christian man is the temple of God; and of a like sort the congregation of the faithful is called the Church of God; and we see that the Pope reigneth in the hearts of some Christian men which worship him even now as their God. And also we see, not only how he reigneth in the hearts of sundry men, but also in the midst of the Church militant as the supreme of all creatures. Therefore it is fully accomplished and performed that spake of him when he wrote that he should sit in the temple, God (not in the temple builded by man's hands at Jerusalem, but in the hearts of men, and in the militant Church of Christ), as though he were God, and braggeth himself before

margin: Dan. vii.

margin: 2 Thess. a ii.

The Tragedy

men as very God. And because these things, which Paul said, cannot be applied to none other in the world, it must of necessity be granted that he only is the same right and great Antichrist, and the very self-same horrible abomination of whom Christ prophesied that he should establish his seat in the Holy Place. Neither was it enough Matt. xxiiii. for him to thrust himself into Christ's place, and to announce himself above God; but also he would deprave the Holy Scriptures, and be in all points quite contrary to Christ. That all these things be true hereof it may appear, even as Christ hath left nothing unprovided for us which are necessary for the maintenance of our natural life, so is it to be believed that much less He would leave any of those necessaries unprovided, which should appertain to the spiritual life.

Therefore must we believe that God hath declared unto us in the Holy Scriptures as much as is needful, whereunto no creature must add, neither take away one word, as God by Moses Deut. xii. doth command, for they only be in all points perfect. Therefore Paul writing to Timothy saith, All Scripture inspired from above is profitable to rebuke and amend, to instruct in righteousness, that a man who is dedicate to God may be upright 1 Tim. iv. and perfect in all good works. Then by the doctrine of Paul, it is plain that those things which be contained in the Holy Scripture be sufficient to

The Tragedy

make a man perfect; which thing must needs be granted, for Christ disclosed to His apostles, as to His beloved friends and children, all that He received of His Father. And afterward He opened their minds by His Spirit, and declared unto them the true meaning of those things which the same apostles did write, preach, and publish abroad plentifully. So that the gospel is most perfect and full, as Paul wrote to the Hebrews. And as for the Pope, he is altogether contrary to these things that be spoken. First and foremost he saith that Holy Scripture is imperfect, and is not sufficient to declare fully all matters that belong to salvation; and that he can add unto it, as he hath done, when he allowed those books that be apocryphal, and of none authority, for holy books, as though they were in the canon. And also when he made an innumerable sort of decrees and decretals and commandments of man and articles of our faith. And he saith moreover (though it be closely), that the twelve articles of the faith delivered and preached by the apostles be not sufficient to salvation. And then the apostles be damned, and all Christian men who hath not received the light of the articles, observations, and commandments of the Pope. So that it must follow (in the name of God) that the Popes were wiser than Christ Himself, or at the leastwise were more merciful, because they have opened so

Antichrist saith that the Scripture is insufficient.

Antichrist corrupteth the articles of our faith.

The Tragedy

many things to the world, which be (as they say) necessary to our salvation, and never opened, neither by Christ nor God. But what a mischievous deed is it that all these articles of the faith made by the Pope be altogether repugnant and quite contrary to the articles of the apostles and to all Holy Scripture, as it is well known! For briefly in the Creed and in Holy Scripture it is comprehended that it is God, by whose goodness and grace through Christ (who suffered death for us, who rose again and ascended into heaven, and sitteth on the right hand of God the Father) all creatures must receive salvation, and also feel His plentiful love towards us, through the Holy Ghost; and that he who believeth in Christ shall have life everlasting as He Himself is a witness.

But the contents of the Pope's articles be altogether contrary to this gear, that is to say, That faith in Christ is not sufficient to salvation, and that it is necessary to believe that the Pope hath authority over all. And that we must believe according to the doctrine of the Pope, that neither the grace of Christ nor the death of Christ is sufficient to salvation, but that our meritorious works must also of necessity be added, with confession devised by the Pope and his absolutions, pardons, and prayer to saints, and besides all this, the fire of Purgatory. And that the Holy Ghost (as they say) is not enough for the understanding of

The Tragedy

Holy Scripture, and to know the will and pleasure of God; but that the Pope must expound all things. No man can deny but this is a very setting of himself above God. Daniel wrote wonderful learnedly of him, saying that he shall induce men naughtily and wickedly to break their promises that they have made to God. For even as God, who is the wellspring of all goodness, promised in Abraham to be our God, that He would take the charge of every one of us, and would give Himself for us, making us partakers of all His felicity; and we again have promised Him that we will be His people, to ask and look for all goodness at His hand only, to acknowledge Him only our God, and will give thanks, and render honour and worship to Him alone: On the other side, the Pope sayeth to this gear, That God is angry with us, and that Christ could not sufficiently pacify His wrath; but that the Pope must help with his authority, and the saints with their prayers and merits, and also we ourselves with our good works, and also the devils with their fire of Purgatory. Therefore is it very true that Daniel said, that he should change the times (he should transpose the time of grace into the time of the law, the time of light into the time of darkness). Neither think they it a deed mischievous enough to make new articles of the faith, at their pleasure contrary to the articles of

Dan. xi.

The Tragedy

God, except also they deprave the law of God with their precepts and commandments, which commandments be also contrary to the commandments of God. For it is without controversy that all the law of God doth depend upon the love towards God and towards our neighbour; and the Pope, minding to destroy both the parts of the law of God, hath infected purposely these two chief grounds upon the which hang all the law and the prophets. For he affirmeth contrary to the express word of God, that God requireth not necessarily of us that we should love Him with all our heart, with all our soul, and all our mind; but that we should love Him above all other things, affirming that to be the commandment; and to love God with all our hearts is but a counsel. And as touching our neighbour, of a like sort he saith, that it is a counsel and a perfection, and not commandment, to love our enemy with all our heart; but that only we ought to show outward tokens of love towards our enemies. And again, whereas the law is most perfect, there, saith he, that it is imperfect, and therefore he holdeth that it is lawful, and that we ought to add something unto it, and to do some works besides them that be commanded in the law of God, which he called supererogatory works, that is to say, works which be not commanded. For this cause hath he delivered new rules to the world, new

Antichrist corrupteth the laws of God.

The Tragedy

trades of living, ordinances, and commandments such (it may chance) as he dreamed when he was in some frenzy; utterly pugnant[1] and contrary to the commandments of God, whereas God commandeth Himself only to be worshipped; he will also be worshipped of us, and moreover com-

Exodus xx. mandeth us that we shall not only worship saints, but also their dead bodies and relics. God willeth and commandeth us that we shall make no image, neither of Himself, neither of any other creature, any picture of similitude to be worshipped. The Pope willeth and commandeth images and pictures of saints to be made, to be set up all about in the church in every corner, there to be worshipped that no place there be void of idolatry. Of a like sort God commandeth that no man should take His name in vain, that is to say, when a man promiseth anything, by an oath taking God to witness, he must keep the thing that he promiseth. But the Pope denieth that promises ought to be kept with heretics (as he taketh heretics), that is to say, with true Christian men, willing and commanding with express words to deceive them, that they may be betrayed, and burned, though he have sworn the contrary never so much, taking God and all saints to witness. Yea, he doth pardon, forgive, and absolve men from their rightful oaths in honest civil matters, so that it redound to his

[1] *Pugnant*, opposed.

The Tragedy

profit and glory, and that he be rewarded liberally therefore. God commandeth the Sabbath day to be kept holy; and since Jesus Christ, the Sun of Righteousness, appeared to the world, we ought to judge all times of grace to be a most Holy Sabbath, and to take all the times of our life, without putting diversity between one day and another, to be altogether holy, and to spend altogether in the honour and glory of God. But the Pope commandeth the contrary, that there shall be a diversity between days and times in holiness, that some days shall be hallowed, yet with none other kind of religion but idleness, idolatry, and superstition, in the remembrance of some feast devised by him, or of some saint that he hath canonised; all other times he taketh not to be holy. God commandeth honour to be given to the father and mother, and obedience to princes, which be ordained of Him. The Pope contrariwise willeth that the children may, contrary to the minds of their parents, profess some superstitious and devilish kind of religion, and remain tied therein to their wicked vows; yea, though their father and mother pine for hunger, and want the comfort of their children by the reason of extreme necessity. He will also have all his priests, monks, and nuns to be free, and discharged from all obedience to their prince and magistrates which be ordained of God. God commandeth that no man

Romans xiii.

The Tragedy

shall kill; but this bloody parricide and mankiller, being made drunk with the blood of martyrs and of Christian men, granteth full pardon to mankillers and parricides, and to such as say they fought under the banner of the cross of Christ; that by the means of this devilish license he may increase and amplify his cruel tyranny. God forbiddeth adultery and all uncleanness, and commandeth, by the mouth of Paul, him who hath not the gift of chastity to marry a wife; but this shameless bawd doth the contrary. He forbiddeth marriage to all that be anointed of him, whether they have the gift of chastity or not, as though marriage were an unholy and an unclean thing, and not much more holy and more honest than is their wifeless life, and as though, according to the doctrine of Paul, matrimony were not honourable, holy, and undefiled in all states. Yet in the mean space he granteth to such as hang upon him all kinds of beastliness and filthy uncleanness. And also at sundry times of the year and within sundry degrees devised by him, he forbiddeth marriage for none other intent but to keep his honour in estimation, and to get great sums of money by dispensing therewith. God commandeth that no man shall desire another man's goods, but this thief, under the pretence of annates,[1]

1 Cor. vii.

---

[1] *Annates*, the first-fruits of benefices, supplied now in the main by "Peter's pence."

The Tragedy

dimes,[1] pardons, jubilees, compositions, absolutions, dispensations, privileges, blessings, grievous and devilish coactions;[2] he overrunneth and robbeth all the whole world. And as soon as these goods be gotten, or rather stolen together, come he by them by robbing or stealing never so, yet be they straightway made holy, and so holy that they may not be alienated without this thief's license. But why stand I so long in this matter? For to knit up so great a matter in few words, whereas Christ came not to break the law, but rather to fulfil it, he corruptly infected and depraved all the whole law. Whereas Christ did abrogate the ceremonial precepts of the Jews, he hath brought in all the devilish superstitions of the Gentiles. Therefore is that undoubtedly true that Daniel spake of him, that he should change the laws. And he is not content to profess openly that the merits of Christ be not enough, and that he fulfilleth the thing that wanteth in them, except he may further have his saying that he is the steward and distributor of the same merits of Christ, and that it is his office to apply them for the quick and the dead, as he shall think good. As who should say that Christ cannot apply them, or else that He would not provide for the health of souls, so that there is much more charity in the Pope than in Christ. What needeth so many

Matt. v.

Dan. vii.

---

[1] *Dimes*, tithes or tenths.   [2] *Coaction*, force, compulsion.

The Tragedy

words? Christ never had, nor never shall have, neither was there ever a greater enemy in the world to the Gospel than he is. He hath continued war with them that believe in Christ, and with all that be godly and virtuous, and them he overcometh with deceit and cruelty, as Daniel said of him before. Wherefore we be bound to confess that he is the true great Antichrist himself.

<small>Dan. xi.</small>

PAPISTA. Then erred the councils wherein it was decreed that he should be Pope.

THOMAS, ARCH. That is as much to say as, Then erred the bishops and Pharisees, when they gathered a council together, and determined to crucify Christ. I pray you, doth that seem so strange a thing, to confess that they have erred, which be bishops by name only, but in deed tyrants and wolves, and wretched varlets joined together in their sessions[1] only to maintain and stablish their tyranny, wickedly depraving the Word of God. If your councils cannot err, how cometh it to pass that many times one of them hath made contrary laws to another? And if one council be contrary to another, as they be indeed, it must be granted that one of them erred. Whereas they speak purposely of the Pope, the Council of Africa made a law that the Bishop of Rome should not only not be Pope, but also that he ought not to have that name. Then either

---
[1] *Sessions*, councils.

The Tragedy

erred that council, or yours. Truly then will I believe your council is gathered together by the Holy Ghost and erred not when I shall perceive that it was not ruled and led by your sensuality, ambitious seeking of honour, and by gifts and rewards, but by the Word of God. If you would expound the Scriptures to the contempt of yourself, and to the glory of God, I would think the matter might be well taken. But if ye will be the judges of Holy Scripture, and then will expound the same, as your dulness, tyranny, and self-will shall lead you, writhing the Word of God otherwise than the true sense and meaning thereof leadeth you,—to the increasing and establishment of your tyranny, minding to usurp the dominion of earth, heaven, and hell, that ye may be worshipped in earth as gods, to the great rebuke of God,—I doubt not but that you are gathered together in the spirit of the devil. And you intend to prove to me the Pope to be Pope by authority of the council. But those things that be established in the council (as you say) be of none effect unless the Pope confirm them. But the Pope cannot confirm them unless he first be Pope. Therefore tell me first, how the Bishop of Rome was made Pope, and how he cannot err in confirming the decrees of the councils, and then may ye prove the popeship by the councils; for otherwise is your argument plain false, or at the least way so

The Tragedy

made in a circle, that in disputation it beginneth again where it began before to no purpose.

PAPISTA. If it were so that the Bishop of Rome were Antichrist indeed, as you say, yet forasmuch as he hath been accounted of Christian men for Pope so many hundred years, and the chief Bishop of all other, then the Church of Christ hath decayed long agone, contrary to His promise who said, I am with you to the world's end.

THOMAS, ARCH. As touching this point the same answer shall be made to you now that was made in time past to Elias, when he thought none alive to embrace the faith of God but himself alone, to whom God said, I have preserved to myself seven thousand who hath not bowed their knees before Baal. Even so is it now; for in Europe, Africa, and Asia, there were always many Christian men who worshipped not Antichrist.

PAPISTA. What! were they all heretics?

THOMAS, ARCH. They were by your saying, for they would neither obey Antichrist, neither believe Purgatory, neither would they keep the feast of Easter upon the Sunday.[1]

---

[1] In the second century arose a dispute about the proper time for celebrating Easter; the Eastern Christians, for the most part, keeping it on the 14th day of the first Jewish month, considering it equivalent to the Passover, while the Western Churches, regarding it as a feast held in honour of the resurrection of Christ, ordered it to be kept on the Sunday after the 14th.

The Tragedy

Henry. Ye have reasoned now enough and enough. Now we see plainly that this fellow, of whom we moved this question, was and is very right Antichrist. From henceforth we will in no wise consent to his evilness lest God continue His anger against us. We have suffered too long a great deal so intolerable a tyranny. We will prove surely whether he be god in the earth or not; and whether we have more full authority in our own dominions and kingdoms than he hath or not.

Papista. Then shall your Majesty lose your title of Defender of the Faith.

Henry. Nay; we will be called the destroyers of the false faith of Antichrist, and maintainers of the true faith of Christ.

IX

KING EDWARD THE SIXTH, THE LORD PROTECTOR [1]

EDWARD. Alexander the Great did set so much by the honour and glory of the world, that when his father Philip overcame more and more cities and countries daily, and all other men rejoiced very much of his victories, yet he alone, being of tender age, lamented very much therefore (notwithstanding that he ought to have been joyful and glad, being his father's only heir of all his kingdoms), thinking that his father would prevent him, and take away all occasion from him, whereby he might compass the dominion of the world by his own wit and industry, whereof should ensue worthy renown and immortal memory, esteeming a kingdom as nothing without glory. But forasmuch as it hath pleased God to lighten our mind with the clear brightness of heavenly doctrine, and thereby

---

[1] In the other copy of this play that is in the British Museum the "Lord Protector" is cancelled and replaced by "The Councillors," unless, indeed, it has been added, taking the place of "The Councillors."

The Tragedy

to give us knowledge that He hath placed us in this seat of a king, that we should direct the use of our sceptre royal, and the stern of our government, not to the glory of the world, but to the glory of Him; so much more we be studious of the glory of God above that the glory of the world, as we know that the one is heavenly, excellent, and durable, and the other vain, sliding away, and able to continue but for a while. And we cannot but lament even from the bottom of our heart, even in this tender age of ours, when we see our only Lord and Saviour, Jesus Christ, with no small rebuke of His Heavenly and Eternal Father, driven out of His seat and kingdom; and such a cruel and wicked tyrant placed in His room. Wherefore we be very desireful to restore Christ into His own former place again, that by Him God may be honoured; not minding in anywise to suffer such abominations to remain within our dominions. All Christian men have evermore abhorred the name of Antichrist; and shall we have him at home with us, knowing him to be such a one as he is, and shall leave him unbanished out of the coasts of our country? That shall never be. Surely all the treasures, honours, friendships, pleasures, and all the happy conditions of this world can never make us happy; no, not so much as in this life; so long as we see not Christ Himself, and not Antichrist, reign in the hearts of His subjects.

The Tragedy

The Majesty Royal of King Henry the Eighth, of famous memory, our natural[1] father, began this worthy and noble enterprise, that we intend, whose steps we will follow for the performance of his will, seeing that he, being prevented with death, could not bring that thing to such perfect end as his mind was at the first attempting thereof. We have determined therefore to pursue the famous enterprise of our most famous father, and not only to pluck up by the roots and utterly banish out of our kingdom the name of Antichrist, and his jurisdiction, but also clearly to purge the minds of our subjects from all wicked idolatry, heresy, and superstition, and such like devilishness as by him was brought in. And forasmuch as there is none other thing that moveth us thus to do, but the only glory of God, we doubt not but that Christ will be with us, and will rule our councils and doings with His Holy Spirit. And although I doubt not but that you study likewise with an earnest ferventness of spirit to set forth this high glory of God, yet have we thought good to disclose this our intent and purpose to you, being our dearly beloved and faithful councillors, to the intent that this godly deed may be the more speedily brought to pass.

---

[1] *Natural father* is used here not in its modern sense of father of an illegitimate child, but simply means "*kind*." The contemporaries of Ben Jonson and Shakespeare constantly used *natural* in the sense of *kind*.

The Tragedy

COUNCILLORS.[1] Surely your Majesty could have told us nothing that could have pleased us better, either that can be more to the glory of God, more profitable to the commonwealth, or else more worthy and honourable to a Christian king. Wherefore we be compelled to render immortal thanks to God, and having a taste of your Grace's wisdom by this thing, to hope for greater and more excellent enterprises of you than any man would conceive, in that we perceive so much sage and ancient wisdom in this your so tender age, and so fervent a zeal to the setting forth of God's glory. For this thing is commonly seen, by the common course of nature, that such men as be of the common sort, and of slender courage, be cold and slack in the way of the Lord; yea, and be many times offended with such a confusion and variety of judgments when they see noble men so carried with a blind and a wicked zeal, with all that ever they can make for the defence of wicked Babylon and of their devilish Antichrist, not staying,[2] with bloody hands and bloody hearts, to be glutted and made drunk with the blood of Christ and of His elects; and many times also have they the better hand, as the heavenly prophet Daniel prophesied. But your

---

[1] In this copy, though the Lord Protector is named as one of the *dramatis personæ*, the "Councillors" alone are they who speak, as in the other copy of this play.   [2] *Staying*, ceasing.

The Tragedy

princely Majesty, as one endued with a high and a heavenly courage, have intended a glorious enterprise, and that being stirred up and inflamed thereunto with a fervent zeal to the glory of God, and ye have taken upon you the cause of Christ and His elects against all the enemies of God. Neither can there be any more worthy means devised to set forth both the glory of God and also of your most excellent Majesty. And it is not to be doubted but that God will use your Majesty as a heavenly mean, and a faultless instrument, to overthrow His great enemy, even as in times past He used David for an instrument to overthrow Goliath. Your Majesty may strike off his head as David, Goliath's, even with his own sword, that is to say, with the Word of God, which he hath made filthily abused in despite of Christ. There were verily not a few of the old emperors who attempted the putting down of this tyranny, and Henry the Fourth and Fifth, Lewis the Fourth, Frederick the First and Second, and many more, who could not overcome him, because he reigned in the minds of men, and the people took him for their god in earth. They feared his thunderbolts and excommunications; they thought themselves damned if they contraried him never so little, and therefore could they not, in good earnest, put on their harness and take their weapons, with a valiant courage of spirit, to deliver

The Tragedy

the Christian commonwealth from this so great a tyranny.

EDWARD. If we mind to overcome him in short space, we must first go about to drive him off the hearts of men; for as soon as he hath once lost his spiritual kingdom in men's consciences, he shall forgo by and by all the rest of his jurisdiction without any great difficulty. And to drive him out of the hearts of men, it is not needful to use sword nor violence. The sword of the Spirit, that is, the Word of God, is sufficient, whereby Christ overcame and conquered His enemy Satan in the desert. For all his whole popeship is nothing else but a manifest deceit and lie. What thing can it be else but a lie to say the Church was builded by Christ upon Peter, and that Peter was instituted by Christ the head of the other apostles and of the Universal Church? And that Cephas in our tongue signifieth a head; and that when Christ said to Peter, Feed my sheep, He made him the only shepherd of souls, and gave to him alone the keys of the kingdom of Heaven, and power to loose and bind? It is also a very vain lie to say Peter was at Rome, and that Peter had authority given him of Christ to leave there, and also that he left there the chief bishop's seat, as in one certain place, there, by succession, continually to remain to the Bishops of Rome (as they hold opinion). It is also a

The Tragedy

manifest lie and deceit to say that Christ is not our only Saviour, Mediator, and Advocate. Purgatory also, devised by them, is a lie, and their lately devised confessions, absolutions, pardons, jubilees, blessings, cursings, and excommunications, be all lies. And also their heresies, hypocrisies, idolatry, promises, flatterings, superstitions, and their devilish and tyrannical authority which they usurp and challenge,[1] with all their whole popehood, be altogether lies. Wherefore seeing the Word of God is a most bright light, at the sight whereof all falsehood and lies be known and avoided, and the truth appeareth invincible, it must needs be, that even as darkness vanisheth away at the sight of the sun, even so at the shining of God's Word, all lies, deceits, treasons, and wickedness of the Pope shall decay, and be utterly plucked up by the roots. This is the spiritual sword by whose edge (as Paul prophesied) he must be slain. Wherefore if we mind to attain honour and glory that never shall perish by this noble enterprise, we must search all about, and get the most faithful ministers of God's Word, which be endued with a great light of the Spirit, in the knowledge and exposition of the Scriptures, with a heavenly eloquence, boldness, and liberty, which ministers both can and will print Christ in the hearts of man. Then without doubt shall Antichrist and

[1] *Challenge*, lay claim to.

The Tragedy

all his whole kingdom be overthrown by and by. This must be our host; these must be our footmen; these must be our horsemen; if we mind to overcome this enemy of God. And if we cannot find enough such men within our own dominions, they must be sought for, wheresoever they may be found; good learning must be made much of, and promoted forward; good wits must be nourished, and provoked to learning and study, that the heavenly philosophy of Christ may reign always in our kingdom. Then surely shall we not be ashamed, when we shall be never so much excommunicated of the wicked Romish robber; but we shall rather rejoice, and with a valiant and bold courage, we shall laugh to scorn his cursings and blessings altogether, not setting a straw by the whole rabble of the rest of his wickedness, his absolutions, dispensations, privileges, bulls, and pardons. Through the sin of our forefather Adam we be naturally so frail and weak, so blind and froward, that we seek for nothing else but our own. Wherefore if we will be moved to set forth and amplify the most high glory of God, it is He that must move and stir us with His heavenly Spirit. And forasmuch as we know, and be very well assured, that all our desire and purposes concerning this matter be bent towards the glory of God, and according to His word, we may be bold to say that this intent of ours is a

The Tragedy

work of God. Therefore even as it cannot be that God will forsake Himself, and leave off to be God; so also can it not be, but that He will triumph over His enemies.

COUNCILLORS. Surely it shall be a very easy thing to obtain what thing soever is godly of your Majesty's subjects. For even, as after the transgression of Adam, God grafted a certain terribleness of countenance in man, whereby he should make beasts afraid with looking upon man, lest they should hurt him; so hath He endowed subjects with a certain natural fear towards their liege lords that they may reverently obey them. Wherefore if a prince or king intend a thing, and then declare the same to be his mind and pleasure with a certain effectualness and authority, by and by they all obey; namely,[1] when he offereth matters unto them that be just and godly. But as for the truth of the doctrine of the Gospel is of itself most effectual, and therefore we doubt not but it will come to pass that it shall gladly be received of all men, especially when it shall be offered unto them of the majesty of a king, and he shall confirm the same with uprightness of life. Neither is it to be doubted that the Gospel should breed any tumult in these dominions, or cause any sedition or looseness of liberty, for Christ doth approve and con-

[1] Particularly.

The Tragedy

firm chiefly the power and authority of princes and magistrates, and causeth men to think humbly and lowly of themselves, and to love peace and quietness; and therefore, as though they were gentle lambs, it shall be an easy thing, and no great pain, to rule them.

EDWARD. We know right well that a sick body which is full of corrupt humours cannot be purged and cleansed without some commotion and stirring of the body and members, and even so is it of our kingdoms. And we also know that the Gospel is a most sweet and pleasant medicine to the chosen of God, although it turn the stomach of such as be rejected. And even as he should not be a good father who, having a son sick that he could make whole again with some medicine, and yet durst not minister the same unto him for fear of stirring of his body, and so suffer his son to perish with the greatness of the disease; so should not we be a good king, if when we see our people sick of a spiritual disease (as indeed we do) should suffer them to perish eternally for fear of a commotion, and should not minister unto them the wholesome medicine of the Gospel whereby to restore them again to health. Wherefore we be in a full readiness to adventure, not only our own honour, but also our life itself for the wealth of our people and for the glory of God. There be not a few that will go about to stay us from

The Tragedy

this noble enterprise. They say that the Greeks, and other nations of the East parts of the world, were punished of God by the tyranny of the Turk, because they refused to obey the Pope. As though the Pope's tyranny were not a great deal greater and crueller than is the tyranny of the Turk. Or as though Africa and Asia had in times past been subject to the Pope. Neither mind we to rent or loose the seamless coat of Christ, as some peradventure will think, who hath cut it into so many small pieces that it can be divided no more. But we mind to cut and tear asunder the veil of hypocrisy, that their vice and wickedness may be known of all men. This thing is without question : As often as ever the Turk hath fought with the Christian men, for the most part he hath had the over[1] hand, which God suffered so to be ; not only to punish us for that instead of Christ, we have worshipped Antichrist, but also because He minded by little and little to withdraw us, and deliver us from the wicked tyranny of Antichrist. And it is not to be doubted but that even as the Jews be punished chiefly for the sins of their priests, because they were the causers of the death of Christ, so be the Christian men punished this day for the sins of Antichrist and his priests, who have crucified Christ again much more in despite of God, than the Jews did in times past. Wherefore if we

[1] *Over*, upper.

The Tragedy

will prevail against the Turk, first let us thrust this wicked man out of the Church of God, which is a home-dwelling Turk, for whose sins God, being offended with us, useth that whip for the punishment of the Christians; and when God is once pleased and contented again with us, we shall easily, by God's help, give him the overthrow. Therefore let us drive all heresy, idolatry, superstition, and wickedness out of the Church of God; and then shall we not only triumph over the Turks, but also they will be converted to Christ, when they shall see the beams of the light of the Gospel, and the holy life of the Christians spread over all. This arrant thief of Rome hath robbed the world under the pretence of religion, and battle against the Turks, and to deliver the Christians which be amongst the Turks in servitude and bondage. Let him now drive himself out of the Church of God, if he mind to deliver us out of bondage, which is much more cruel and tyrannical than the other. Let him drive Satan out of himself and out of his wicked Babylon, and then being converted and armed with spiritual virtues and with the sword of God's Word, following the example of Christ and His apostles, let him fight against God's enemies. And if it so be that he cannot be amended, but will continue on still in his wicked and cruel tyranny, so that he will compel force to be made, let it be made

The Tragedy

against him; for he only noyeth[1] more the Church of Christ than all the enemies of God joined together. We hate not the Pope's person, but his abominations, whom all men ought of duty to abhor.

COUNCILLORS. Even as the doctrine of the Gospel excelleth all kinds of learning in pureness, gentleness, pleasantness, profitableness, excellence, and wonderfulness; so if it be infected once with never so little an heresy, it is more pestilent and pernicious than any other. Wherefore let us do all our endeavours that it, being purged from all false and superstitious imaginations and man's traditions, may be ministered to the people pure, simple, and sincere, as it is of itself. And as concerning the articles of the faith, the Word of God ought to be sufficient, except we will seem wiser than God Himself. And as touching works, the law that God Himself hath made, which is most pure and holy, shall be sufficient; whose precepts be without spot; sound, and cheerful to the mind; whereunto Christ's interpretation must be annexed. And as for prayer and invocation, what shall we rather allow than the Lord's Prayer, which the Son of God Himself taught us? Which teacheth us plainly and fully what we ought to ask of God; and it also teacheth how we ought to ask all gifts of God through Christ,

---

[1] *Noyeth*, injureth or afflicteth.

The Tragedy

our Mediator. Forsooth, it is a wicked thing to desire to be more wise than was Christ Himself, who delivered us that prayer as a perfect form of prayer; wherefore it cannot be well to add anything thereunto. Truly all doctrine, that is necessary for salvation, is plain and clear, if we darken it not with the darkness of man's inventions. We will therefore do our diligence, first to put away all such things as may be a hindrance to the going forward of the Gospel; and having always God's honour before our eyes, and the health of souls, we will pray that He will grant unto us that pureness and earnestness of spirit, that we may set forth His glory and serve Him in holiness, and that we may, through Jesus Christ our Redeemer, give all praise, glory, and honour to God the Father everlasting. Amen.

THE END

Imprinted at London for G. Walter Lynne, dwelling on Somers Keye, by Byllynges Gate.

Cum privilegio ad imprimendum solum.

Anno Do. 1549.

www.ingramcontent.com/pod-product-compliance
Lightning Source LLC
Chambersburg PA
CBHW031941230426

43672CB00010B/2001